Is it still raining in Aberfan?

Satellites and Sunglasses, Merthyr Vale, 1990

Is it still raining in Aberfan?

A Pit and its People

by
Melanie Doel & Martin Dunkerton

Logaston Press
1991

LOGASTON PRESS
Little Logaston Woonton Almeley
Herefordshire HR3 6QH

First published by Logaston Press 1991
© Copyright Melanie Doel
(text where not otherwise acknowledged)
© Copyright Martin Dunkerton
(photographs where not otherwise acknowledged)

ISBN 0 9510242 9 9

Set in Frutiger by Logaston Press
Printed in Great Britain by
Butler & Tanner Ltd, Frome and London

CONTENTS

Acknowledgements

Our first thanks go to everyone interviewed in this book, especially the following for their help in research: Bill King, Tony Davies, Peter Evans, Russell John, Graham Schewitz, Dr. Arthur Jones, Mike Meredith and Gaynor Madgewick.

We would also like to thank the members of the Merthyr Vale lodge of the NUM, especially their chairman Ivor John, his wife Mary and their two sons for all their kindness and help.

Special mention must also be made of Robert Haines for his invaluable research work and encouragement; Clive Thomas for his invaluable help and support; Mr. Eddie John; Merthyr Tydfil Borough Council; staff at Merthyr Library, in particular Carolyn Jacobs, and for allowing reproduction of the photographs on pages 10 and 18; The Cyfarthfa Museum in Merthyr; also The Industrial and Maritime Museum in Cardiff and in particular for allowing reproduction of the photographs on pages 12, 28 and 34; of The Times Newspaper for allowing us to use the left-hand photograph on page 46 (taken by Melville Parry, aged 18 with his first photo on his first roll of film!); The Oxford Mail for the photograph of Gerald & Sylvia Williams and those on pages 70 and 71; of Kim Howells for the bottom two photographs on page 67; of Jeremy Nicholl for the photograph on page 82, of British Coal for the photographs on pages 52 and 58 and of the portrait of Graham Schewitz; of the Press Association for the photographs on pages 36, 44, 45, 46 (right), 48, 67 (top right) and 81; of Steve Wolstencroft for the maps; of Dan Griffiths and pupils from Ynysowen Primary School, and of Mr. Bryn Carpenter.

Thanks also to Eben Morris for allowing reproduction of part of The Angry Summer by his brother-in-law Idris Davies.

Also to everyone else who has been involved in the book's content and production without whose goodwill, advice and encouragement it would never have seen the light of day. Finally to Andy Johnson of Logaston Press for bringing it all together.

Melanie Doel & Martin Dunkerton
September 1991

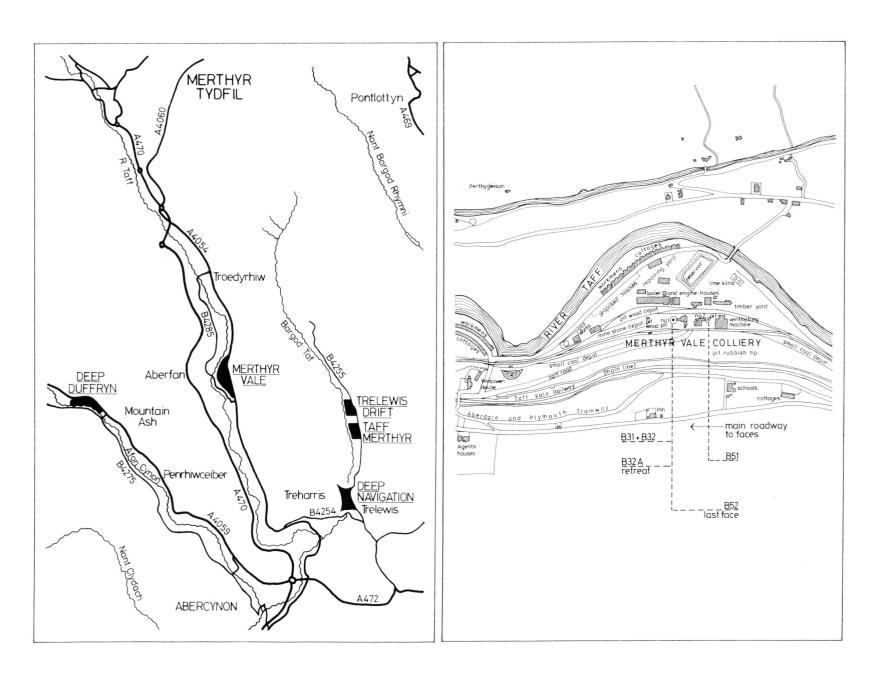

Left: The Merthyr area and its longest surviving pits   Right: Merthyr Vale 1882, with the approximate position of later coal faces

Taff Merthyr Colliery, Treharris, 1990

Foreword

The name 'Aberfan' will always have a special significance because of the terrible tragedy that robbed the village of a generation of school children.

In this book Melanie Doel not only writes with passion about the disaster that could have been avoided, but Martin Dunkerton has photographed the community and the changes over the last decade. They have also collected the stories of miners and their families recounting their experiences over many years in this Welsh mining village.

Here is an authentic and moving history of life in Aberfan before and after the catastrophe. I recommend it with all my heart.

George Thomas
Viscount Tonypandy

Merthyr Vale colliery looking south, 1880's or 1890's

'Many hills and woods good plenty, though there were some red deer, kids plenty, oxen and sheep' is how John Leland described north Glamorgan on his itinerary in the 1530's. The uplands were well suited to sheep and cattle rearing, whilst cereals were grown in the valleys.

Between the sixteenth and eighteenth centuries agriculture with its scattered farms dominated the economic and social life of the borough with most of the population rearing livestock and producing butter, cheese and wool. Spinning and weaving were commonplace as was the knitting of socks at home for sale at local markets, from where they were exported to Bristol and Maidenhead. Tanning, shoe and glovemaking were other occupations. Drovers frequently passed through the valley from the St Mary Hill Fair near Bridgend to Hereford and London.

But even from the early sixteenth century many farmers had combined agricultural with industrial work, operating small coal workings and lime kilns, providing work for men, horses and candlemakers, as well as for carpenters and blacksmiths manufacturing carts and trams. Coal was obtained by quarrying.

Small ironworks had existed in the Taff valley since Tudor days, however large scale production was prevented by poor communications with only mules and ponies on which to travel. But in the middle of the eighteenth century the increased demand for iron led to improved methods of production using coke instead of charcoal, whilst canals and railways improved the transport network. Geographical conditions in the Merthyr and Heads of the Valleys area were ideal for the new method of production as the raw materials—iron ore, coal and limestone—were easily accessible near the surface.

From 1759 four large ironworks, Dowlais, Cyfarthfa, Plymouth and Penydarren were established within a few years of each other. By 1803 Cyfarthfa had become the largest ironworks in the world with six blast furnaces. The population of Merthyr rose from 700 at the end of the eighteenth century (itself an increase on the 110 of 1660), to 80,000 a century later. Stable employment and high wages acted as a magnet to people from the rural areas of Wales and later Ireland, at a time when life on the land was precarious as severe weather led to poor harvests and famine.

But even by the end of the 1840's it was clear the iron industry could not be sustained. Local ore reserves were practically exhausted and the cost of importing ore made Merthyr iron less competitive. Although the industry continued into the twentieth century, the second half of the nineteenth saw the emphasis switch from iron to coal, and the industrial development of the valley south of Merthyr.

Group of colliers with shovels, late ninteenth or early twentieth century

John Nixon

John Nixon was born in the small village of Barlow in the county of Durham, seven miles west of the thriving industrial area of Newcastle on Tyne, on 10 May 1815. The age of steam and coal had begun in earnest the year before, when George Stephenson had placed the first locomotive on rails at Killingworth.

Nixon's family had little money but he was sent away to Newcastle to be educated at Dr. Bruce's academy which had the reputation for turning out large numbers of highly regarded mining and civil engineers. Robert Stephenson, twelve years older than Nixon, had also been educated there. At fourteen Nixon's short but thorough education came to an end and he was apprenticed to Joseph Gray at Garesfield, one of northern England's leading mining engineers and a mining agent to the Marquis of Bute. It was largely through the Marquis that he obtained a job in Wales, at Dowlais. From there he moved to south-western France, but couldn't see their coal being mined competitively. On his return to England he travelled on a steamer on the Thames. The story continues in the words of James Vincent in his biography of Nixon, Pioneer of the Steam Coal Trade in South Wales, published in 1899.

'The stoker threw coal onto the fire; no volume of black smoke was vomited forth by the funnel. Now, Mr. Nixon ... naturally supposed that the coal in use on a Thames steamer would surely have come from Newcastle. He also knew enough of Newcastle coal to be convinced that, unless it were coaxed with infinite tenderness and subjected to special arrangements for complete combustion, that fuel would certainly not conduct itself in this amiable and pleasing manner. Under ordinary circumstances it would belch forth a cloud of murky smoke. Thereupon Mr. Nixon, always keenly observant ... congratulated the captain in an interrogatory tone, on the excellence of his smoke consuming apparatus. The captain ... bluntly answered that "there was no smoke in the coal."

'Now a fire without smoke was in those days quite as remarkable a thing as smoke without a fire, and the captain's reply served to set Mr. Nixon's intelligent curiosity more awake than ever. ... After paying half a crown for the privilege of throwing some of the coal on the fire, Mr. Nixon went below.' He asked the stoker from whence it came. 'We get it from Mr. Wood and they call it Murther coal' was the reply which sent Nixon back to Wales.

Anticipating demand from Europe from his brief work there, he immediately sought out Mr. Wood. But Wood had no interest in expanding, saying he would only sell two boat loads a day from Wales and for which he already had a market. Giving up on Wood he went to Cardiff to see a Mr. Marychurch who had coal for sale. Marychurch stated that he had little coal to spare since all he could obtain was sold in London. However he did inform Nixon that his supplies came from the Graig pit, Waun-y-wyllt, at Merthyr, the property of Mrs. Thomas.

Mrs. Thomas was a remarkable character. 'She may be called the mother of the coal trade. ... She sat in her office, a wooden hut near the pit's mouth, and traded for cash, placing in a basket over her head the moneys which she received for her coal. Her cleverness, her witty tongue, her pleasant manner were well known to all the countryside. At the pit's mouth it may be said that the poetry of the arcadian world joined hands with the prose of a busier time come. "Laughing girls" like those who trod the wine press of old (save they were grimy with coal dust) handled the coal, sorting it out by hand and picking out the lumps, which were afterwards placed on boats as carefully as if each lump were an egg and Mrs. Thomas was then raising the amount, considerable in those days, of one hundred and fifty tons a day.'

She refused to produce more to supply him, saying it was already appalling the amount she was taking from the bowels of the earth, a common fear then and later in the Welsh coalfield.

Nixon continued to travel between Wales, northern England and France and eventually learnt that a Mr. Powell had sunk down to excellent steam coal in the Aberdare valley. Here at last was a man needing a market for his coal. Nixon wasted no time in visiting Powell's number one pit at Abernant-y-groes where he found he was already producing 150 tons a day and was on the point of establishing a new pit. Powell listened intently to Nixon's ideas and took him on as a salesman. Nixon chartered a vessel, loaded it with 100 tons of coal, and took it to Nantes where he used his old contacts and arranged a test for his coal in a sugar refinery.

'To the man familiar with coal from the north of England, painfully acquainted with the constantly recurring necessity for stirring up the fire and for cleaning out the entire furnace, Welsh steam coal is puzzling at the outset. The action is too simple: it burns away steadily, and without effort on the part of the stoker. If it is poked and raked and meddled with, it burns away too fiercely, and, to use vulgar but expressive language, plays the mischief with the furnace and burns away the bars.' With the Newcastle coal then in use work had to be interrupted to remove the scoria from the furnaces, but now 'ten hours of fire from the Aberdare valley were unquestionably proved to be worth twelve hours of fire imported from Tyneside.'

With orders from the refineries, and then from the French navy, Nixon decided he needed his own supply. For once fortune was on his side for he was hired to survey the quality of the coal reserves at Werfa which were being worked by the Aberdare Company at Abernant. He found extra supplies of coal just outside the boundary of the Werfa mine and applied to the Marquis of Bute's agents to lease the land.

Finances were often fraught and he was often on the brink of bankruptcy, but gradually he met the right business partners and slowly accumulated additional funds to invest. With William Cory he opened a colliery at Aberdare which was to become deeper than any other colliery previously sunk in South Wales. They leased a large tract of minerals and christened it Navigation Colliery a name soon to become synonymous with good quality coal. Acquisition of Deep Duffryn followed and then he turned his eye to the Merthyr valley.

'Far beneath the surface of the Merthyr valley, some miles to the southward of any coal that had been proved in the district, and to the deep of the coal hitherto worked, a large tract of coal was believed to lie. It had attracted the notice of others before Mr. Nixon turned his attention to it. For example, Mr. Tom Powell, one of the largest coal owners in the district had desired to sink down to it, but his brothers and partners had positively declined to face the enormous outlay, which was an unavoidable preliminary to winning the coal.' But Nixon was more determined.

'In the course of the tedious operation of sinking the men struck into a mass of running silt, which may be taken to be as troublesome an obstacle as the sinkers of pits can encounter. First they tried ... a north of England device ... with four suspended side walls of timber to prevent the silt from running in. Twenty yards were accomplished in this way, but after that relentless nature vanquished man, and the whole apparatus collapsed. Others were for yielding on the spot and for commencing operations elsewhere. But that was not Mr. Nixon's spirit. ... he availed himself of material which lay under his eye, and was to be obtained at small expense. He had observed, lying by the railway hard by, a quantity of worn out Barlow rails belonging to the Great Western Railway Company. These he bought at £3 a ton. Of these he drove into position a sufficient number to form a complete casing to the pit.' This was repeated every 6 feet down until hard rock was reached, requiring yet more time to penetrate. 'Five weary years of labour, of struggling against the force of nature, of expenditure which must long remain unremunerative, passed away before the valuable coal was struck and the pit became a rich colliery, fitted with the most expensive and effectual machines, and equipped with patent ventilating apparatus which was among the most useful of Mr. Nixon's many inventions.' This equipment was also installed in the House of Commons.

In a time of such fast progress it was inevitable that there would be disputes between Nixon and his men. At Deep Duffryn there were complaints about the croppers. It was the cropper's job to assess the amount of small coal, stones or rubbish that was brought to the surface by a miner, miners receiving higher pay for large coal, and less for the small which was, in those days, virtually useless. As a result the croppers were hated by most men and accused of favouring their friends.

'Hardly a day passed without angry remonstrance, and many temporary strikes occurred. At last things came to a climax. On the Monday morning following a Saturday pay day Mr. Nixon went up to the colliery. Instead of industry he found idleness. The winding engines were not at work; the men, instead of being engaged in winning the coal from the depths of the earth, were playing upon the surface. A conversation with his manager soon placed him in possession of the facts. Pay-day had been too much for the feelings of the men; their indignation against the cropper had passed from words to open violence, and they had pitched him neck and crop into the canal. Monday morning had come and no man could be found to take the cropper's bishopric.'

Nixon suggested making a machine to weigh the coal, but the men were wary of this and instead suggested a new cropper. When still no-one could be found to undertake the job Nixon insisted on the machine, whereupon the miners started a two week strike. At the end of this period they agreed to the machine's introduction, to become known as the Billy Fairplay, and it soon entered into universal use in the South Wales collieries and ironworks.

He also retained his interest in marketing coal and anticipated the need for improved transport systems to ferry the coal to its market. In 1853 he organised a petition in South Wales requesting the Marquis of Bute to provide more suitable dock accommodation at Cardiff, as the original dock was becoming too small to handle the increasing size of ships required to cope with the fourfold increase in the annual tonnage of coal passing through the port. A new dock was duly constructed.

He tried unsuccessfully to restrict output at each pit to try and control prices, but he did create a scheme to periodically fix the price of coal among coal owners and became chairman of the Coal Owners Association where he introduced a sliding scale of pay for miners based on the ease with which coal could be extracted.

Nixon died in 1899, and management of his company passed to his nephew.

The 1926 strike was called against a background of rising unemployment and poverty. In August 1925 there were 1,440,628 people out of work, a rate of about 12 per cent, but the rate amongst miners was 22 per cent.

By October 1925 Merthyr had the fifth highest unemployment rate in Britain at 52.2 per cent. At the time Jarrow lay second in the league with 56 per cent. Coal exports had dropped by a third and prices for the remainder had plummeted. Profits of £50 million in 1923 had been converted into a £7 million loss in 1926.

To try to restore profitability mine owners asked miners to work longer hours for less pay. In April 1926 these negotiations broke down and hundreds of miners were locked out of their place of work.

On 4 May the TUC called a national trade union strike in support of the miners demands for a living wage. Nine days later the general council of the TUC, despite opposition from the Labour Party, called off the strike following a series of talks with Stanley Baldwin's government. They were concerned that a continuation would threaten the union movement and could also cause severe financial problems for the TUC. In calling off the action they claimed the strike had not failed and that negotiations could continue.

However the miners continued their strike, receiving more than £1.2 million from Russian miners and trade unions. As the bitterness and repression grew over the summer and then autumn, more and more men and women were arrested in disturbances and demonstrations. Even the publishing and handling of literature became a crime. Many were sentenced to months of hard labour.

To retain morale, a resilient alternative culture sprang up in the valleys with jazz and comic bands being formed, much to the anger of local church leaders who saw them as a spiritual threat.

A war of attrition developed with the government lasting until 1 December when the miners were forced to accept lower wages and longer hours. The Fed, or Miners Federation, was shattered for nearly a decade, lodge officials and activists were victimised and blacklists created. A rival scab union called the South Wales Miners Industrial Union was formed, whilst many miners started to migrate from the valleys.

The communities suffered even more. The period after the strike saw a lessening of colliery customs, whilst chapels, football teams and mining institutes and their libraries went into a dramatic decline. By April 1928 there were 70,000 unemployed in the coal industry in South Wales and 56 collieries closed between the start of 1927 and April 1928. It was to bear an uncanny resemblance to 1984.

Aberfan Road, Aberfan

18

Bill and Bet Carey

Bill Carey was born in 1910, started work in 1924 and retired in 1971, having been on light duties at the pit since being buried in a fall on 12 December 1963. His brother, Donald, died ten years ago from illness caused by the mine's dust. His wife Bet's family, like his own, had come from Ireland looking for work.

When the pit was sunk and the community started to develop around it many people fled the poverty of Ireland to find work at Merthyr Vale. Bill Carey's father, Patrick, was the eldest of nine children living in a tiny cottage at Skibbereen in County Cork. His family scratched a living off the land, cooking on a stone hearth and with the entire family living in one room downstairs and just two small bedrooms. The land around the cottage was little more than rocks and peat and the family struggled to survive growing potatoes. Hungry and desperate for work at the age of 16 in 1901 he decided to seek his fortune in Wales.

'It took him several days to walk from Skibbereen to Cork harbour, finding very little food to keep him going. Stowing away in a cattle ship he made the rough crossing from Cork to Fishguard, constantly hiding from the crew.

'When he arrived in Aberfan he first took up lodgings in a terraced house in The Grove and although as a miner he was earning a wage for the first time in his life, he wasn't earning enough to send any money home.'

Three years later Patrick married Annie Evans, a young girl whose family had moved to Merthyr Vale from Penygroes in North Wales, also for the work. He faced an immediate language barrier for her family was entirely Welsh speaking, not one of them being able to hold a conversation in English. Annie quickly picked up the language, but her mother never spoke English properly until the day she died.

The couple had seven children before Patrick died at the age of 51, Bill being the oldest boy out of the seven children. Bill remembers that when he started work years ago there were few alternatives, and he and his brother were destined to a life in the pit, work for which his father had travelled from Ireland to seek.

'I hadn't had any education to speak of, although I went to school until I was 14, and I thought it was clever to work in the pit. Like all the other boys in the street, I wanted to go down to show I was a man.

'There wasn't anything else to do anyway, practically every one of my schoolmates joined me except the sons of shopkeepers, the lucky ones who were able to go into the family business to help their fathers.

'I can remember my first pay, two shillings and six pence a day, and we worked forty-eight hours a week on a six day week. When I started work in the number two pit there must have been at least 300 of us working in just that one pit at each shift. It all came as a bit of a shock as I went down in the cage that first time. But I loved it. I soon came to realise the truth in the old miners' saying that in the winter you didn't get to see daylight unless you were brought home on a stretcher.

'I'd go out in the dark and come home in the dark walking along cold streets lit only by a gas lamp. But there would be lots of us. As I came out of my house I'd join a stream of men all going into work. The hob nail boots would make a lovely sound as we walked down the street, all dressed in our oldest clothes, unless we were lucky to have afforded moleskin trousers bought from Cardiff or Pontypridd. Under my arm would be a three pint can of water and a couple of jam sandwiches. When you got to work there were so many going underground in those days that you'd have to queue to go down in the cage.

'I wasn't frightened and it was a big adventure. It was very hot—some of the workers would strip right down and work in their underpants because the ventillation was very poor. The air would go down a shaft in one pit and up through the other, and by the time it had travelled all round it was very warm with little oxygen. There was also water coming from Penydarren further north so it would be very wet.

'As a boy I had to work the curling boxes, boxes used to carry the coal worked by the collier to the trams. All day I'd scurry back and fore with the boxes full of coal. When you sat down to eat there were mice and cockroaches everywhere. You'd open your box and they'd suddenly appear and you had to fight for your life to keep them off your food.'

During the 1926 strike Bill and his father went to work on a relative's farm outside Bristol to try to keep some money coming into the house.

'People would organise their own entertainment and there was something on in the village every night. There were such a lot of unemployed in the village that the strike didn't really seem to make all that much difference; a lot of people hadn't been able to get work for a long time anyway so everybody was poor. At the time it seemed 50 per cent of the village was out of work and living on starvation levels.'

Bill also remembers the later poverty of the 30's and 40's. 'It was terrible for the housewife. How they made ends meet I'll never know, as it was a worry for them all the time. Everybody had tick in the shop. You'd have your goods a little bit at a time every day and you'd pay on Friday, and sometimes the pay didn't cover the things you'd bought. Everything was on the never never and you bought what you could, knowing you had to settle up on a Friday.

'But we never went hungry. We'd have broth made from vegetables, and bread pudding—good wholesome food. My family was really lucky because my father always kept pigs and chickens in Cottrell Street. My father would feed the pigs in the night but once I got home from the pit it was my job to feed them. I'd go around with a barrow to all the neighbours picking up the scraps, peelings and bits of vegetables, and would boil them up in the shed. When the pig was ready we'd pay Mr. Salter to take him to the local slaughter house in Aberfan. We always had a side of bacon hanging up in the kitchen—we were considered quite posh. We also had ducks and chickens so we were always eating eggs. When it came to eat the birds my father would kill them with a penknife.'

His wife Bet remembers how families would be subjected to visits from government workers. 'The men were supposed to spend their whole day looking for work if they were unemployed. If the inspector called to the house and found him not looking, the small payments families were receiving could stop.

'I remember how whenever there was a knock on the door my mother would send me, as a small girl, to the door and like all the children I was trained to say "my father's not here he's out trying to find a job." Can you imagine how they wanted the men who had virtually no shoes on their feet and had had hardly anything to eat, to tramp around the valleys looking for work?'

Bet used to be sent to the corner shop or local co-op every day to do the shopping. 'I always remember having to ask for Sunlight soap. I'd also be sent for things like a pound of sugar from the sack on the floor, a couple of ounces of tea and a half a pound of butter. When my mother spread the butter on our bread she'd run the knife over twice. Once to put some butter on and then back again to try to scrape off as much as possible to save money.'

As one of six children supported by a father who was severely crippled by arthritis, Bet soon became the pride of her family when she won a scholarship to the Quakers Yard grammar school a few miles away.

'We couldn't afford the uniform, but I was lucky to find a girl who was leaving and who was about my size and we managed to find ten shillings to buy her gymslip, hat and satchel.' But despite her education there was no way she could go to college. She left school at 16 and when her father later became the steward of the Ex-Servicemen's Club, or The Daggers as it was known, she went to work there

Idris Davies was born in the Gwent town of Rhymney in 1905. For seven years he worked underground as a miner before attending Loughborough College and Nottingham University and qualifying as a teacher. During the Second World War he taught mainly in the London area before returning to South Wales where he died in 1953.

Now it is May among the mountains,
Days for speeches in the valley towns,
Days of dreams and days of struggle,
Days of bitter denunciation.

Now it is May in all the valleys,
Days of the cuckoo and the hawthorn,
Days for splashing in the mountain
   ponds,
Days for love in crowded parks.

Now it is May in little gardens,
In square allotments across the railway,
Days for song and dance and roaming,
Days for action and achievement.

Now it is May in the minds of men,
Days for vision and for marching,
Days for banners and for music,
And beauty born of sacrifice.

From **The Angry Summer**, a poem of 1926

scrubbing the floors and cleaning the club. Later she went to the ordnance factory in Bridgend to make armaments.

'My childhood in Merthyr Vale was really happy despite the poverty. We'd make a game out of anything. A piece of wood could be used to play Catty and Doggy, marbles was a favourite and we were always skipping—with the men holding the rope. For they would always hang around on street corners smoking half a cigarette, dabbing it out half way through and putting it behind their ears.

'At this time there was great excitement when The Coons band was started up and the men were taught to march. Suddenly they were transformed from corner boys, as we'd call them, into a disciplined and proud bunch of men. They had to practice every night and when they performed they had to black up their faces. Two ladies from the village made their suits, white trousers and a shirt, and they'd pay twopence or threepence a week to join. It was wonderful to see them practising under the eye of a trained guardsman marching and reeling around the Ex-Servicemen's Club. Then they'd go off to the exhibitions and competitions and when they came home all the mothers would be sitting outside, their wooden chairs pulled into the street waiting to see how The Coons had done.'

At about the same time a dispute flared at the colliery over wages and an independent arbitrator, a German businessman, was brought in to mediate, and a strange pay system was eventually agreed. Single men were to earn seven shillings a shift; married men without children seven and threepence and those married with children seven and sixpence. Bill was then a single man. 'I remember people were upset at doing exactly the same work as others and getting much less. It caused quite a few grumbles, but the men accepted it.'

During the war the men working underground were classed as being in reserved occupations as coal was desperately needed, and so missed active service.

Bill and Bet refused to allow their sons underground. Bill explains 'It was not a natural way of life and I didn't want it for my boys. I knew men who were treated like slaves and they're all gone now—dead. They were just like human robots and were all worked out by an early age. I was glad to see the pit closed. It should have closed fifty years ago, that would have saved lots of other children from getting knocked about. Today's children would have been the dust generation of the future—poverty would be better than that. Look at me now, I can hardly cross the road because of the dust in my chest, and what did I get for it, just £600 compensation. I'm glad its gone.'

'These are your children begging for bread,
You foolish miners!' the newspaper said.
'Look at the pictures that all may see—
Victims of your stupidity!
O you stubborn, callous men,
Starving your kids and wives again,
Striking because the weather is fair,
And leaving your collieries out of repair,
And drinking your beer as if you had right
To share in the joy of a summer night.
Once you were heroes, you rescued your kind
Out of the galleries left blazing behind,
And we praised you in eloquent journalese
And chatted about you at parlour teas.
And now you won't work for your daily bread,
You lazy miners!' the newspaper said.

From **The Angry Summer**

Reg Probert

Reg Probert was born in Penrhiwceiber and moved to Aberfan Crescent in 1918 when he was eight years old. More than most he probably has reason to feel bitter about the price his family paid for coal. He was seriously injured in an underground fall and eventually his leg had to be amputated. His mother was killed in the Aberfan disaster, his brother lost two children in the tragedy and his sister also lost a child.

'I was eight years old when the community was hit by the 1926 General Strike. I remember how a soup kitchen was set up in Trinity Chapel not far from our home. Every evening me and my brothers and sisters would go straight there from school with all my friends and classmates. We'd sometimes get jam sandwiches and a cup of tea and occasionally there were corned beef sandwiches and soup. There was very little in the house and without the soup kitchen we wouldn't have had any food after school, though I never remember my mother and father going there.' Pride probably stopped many adults taking the charity of the kitchens.

Two weeks after Reg celebrated his fourteenth birthday he went to work underground at Merthyr Vale colliery, staying there until he joined the army in 1940. But even though he'd managed to obtain work, life was far from settled.

'When I first started there must have been about 600 men working at the pit in three shifts. Of course we had strikes in 1932 and 1933 and it seemed a time when there was a lot of conflict. In 1933 we were often on short time working. I was only getting paid twelve shillings a week and of course I gave all of that to my mother after paying my union dues. But very often you would only work two or three days a week and you'd then be sent home. We used to stand in the yard at the pit waiting for notices about when there next would be work. I remember if you managed to get dole money you'd only get half a crown for the rest of the week.'

Reg joined the Welsh Guards in 1940 and was captured within minutes of arriving at Boulogne in France. 'We'd got less than half a mile when we were halted by German tanks coming down the road. There was nothing we could do as all I had was a rifle and a bayonet. For the next five years I was a prisoner of war, being moved around to various camps in Poland, Germany and Austria until the Yanks rescued us.'

Reg returned to a very different life. 'People suddenly had well paid jobs in the war working in factories and the village was certainly more prosperous. Life was so much better when I returned.'

After spending just a few months recovering back at home in Aberfan, Reg was again forced to look for work and hoped to reap the benefits of some of the new prosperity. But after failing to find work on local building sites and in factories, he was forced underground once again. 'Life in the pit hadn't changed a great deal although things were quicker with more machinery to do the work. It was better than when I'd left. The pay was better too although I was still earning just £5 a week and that included overtime for working on a Sunday.'

In 1947 his mining career was brought to a sudden end in a roof fall. 'I had just sat down with my friend who wanted to have his lunch when the roof crashed down onto my leg smashing both bones.'

Reg was not able to work underground again and was off work until 1955 when he was taken on at the government sponsored Remploy factory in Merthyr which provides work for workers with a disability. He stayed there for 29 years until he retired at the age of 65.

In 1986 doctors decided his leg had to be amputated. 'The maddening thing was that the doctors said the circulation had gone and so it would have to come off. But they said it had nothing to do with the fall underground and I have not been able to claim any compensation.'

Suzie Evans and Doris Richards

Both Suzie and Doris were born in 1903, Suzie in Abercynon where her father was a miner though her mother came from a Herefordshire farming family, whilst Doris was born in Aberfan. Suzie's family soon returned to Merthyr Vale where her father had been born. He contracted malaria during the First World War, from which he later died.

Doris' father worked in a lime kiln in the Merthyr Vale pit yard and her two brothers also worked in the colliery. Both her father-in-law and husband were miners who suffered from dust, her husband William retiring early as a result. Their son Hadyn started in the pit but didn't like the work and left after a short time.

During the 1920's and 1930's villagers from Merthyr Vale and Aberfan suffered extreme poverty. Work, even at the pit, was spasmodic and many were unemployed for years on end. But hardship and strong socialist beliefs bound many of the villagers together. Suzie and Doris, both now aged 88, have remained solid friends since they joined the Labour Party at the same time more than sixty years ago. Until recently Suzie lived in a modern bungalow built on the site of the old pit stables, but now lives with her daughter not far away on the main road.

'Things have changed so much. I remember the days when you wouldn't lock your door day or night—you didn't have to as nobody would dream of coming into your home to steal things. But now it's very different. You have to lock yourself in. It's not the same place.'

She spent much of her life in a block of tenement houses called The Barracks, because of the similarity to army accommodation, built to house the mining families that had flocked to the area looking for work. All her five children were born here.

'There was no bathroom—you had to wash in front of the fire. I can remember how they would only have one pair of knickers and one vest so I'd wash them out and try to dry them every night because I didn't want people to know we only had the one set. There was usually a family of at least eight living in each unit in The Barracks.

'I didn't really get any schooling as I always seemed to be too ill. I was in a sanatorium in Tenby in west Wales for months recovering from TB and I never did learn to read or write. But it didn't seem to worry my parents, for people didn't expect girls to be educated then.' Even now Suzie relies on her life-long friend Doris to read or write any important letters.

'When I was thirteen I was sent away to Park Place in Cardiff to work in service as a parlour maid. I was paid £1 a month and sent half home to my family.'

Like many young girls in the village Suzie was destined to marry a miner and she and her husband Jim suffered with the rest of the community during the 1926 strike. 'I was pregnant and can remember when I used to arrive at the soup kitchen they'd laugh and say "Quick give her the food once she smells it, or she'll pass out." I used to have whatever was going. Sometimes it would be soup, other days a sandwich. Sometimes because I was having a baby they'd put a spoon of Nestlés condensed milk in a cup and put boiling water on it. That was to help feed the baby.

'After the men had finished their meal they'd go up to an old disused drift mine above the valley and would pick coal there to try and keep us warm. Jim got stuck inside more than once. The level had been closed for some time and there were often falls. Once when they were trapped by the roof coming down they had to walk right under the mountain and found an exit in the next valley at Bedlinog. He also went potato picking in Pembrokeshire to try to get money.

'If we wanted to call a meeting or get the community together the women would go out into the street with tins and drums and spoons and bang them together until everyone came out.

'During the strike some of the men would strip down and with chains tied across their bodies would crawl along being whipped as if they were slaves.

Suzie's son Billy says 'When my father was working I remember he used to come home in his dirty clothes and every night would fall asleep in front of the fire. He was exhausted from the work. After an hour or two he would wake up and I would help carry boiling water in kettles from the range to fill the tin bath in front of the fire.'

When in her teens Suzie was able to experience at first-hand the conditions in which the men of the village worked. 'One Sunday young women were allowed to go underground. I decided to go down before I was married when I was about 16. I remember having to put on a big pair of overalls and a helmet, but nothing prepared me for what I was about to see. I was shocked by the conditions in which they were working. I saw men sitting, stripped to the waist and with cockroaches around them as they ate their lunch from their tommy boxes.'

The cockroaches, and other smaller bugs known locally as black bats, didn't just stay in the pit. Doris remembers 'Sometimes you'd open the tommy box when the men came home at night and find a cockroach in there. It was horrible—they were huge. Other times the men would have sweated so much during their work that when they changed to come home they would roll up their soaking wet vest and put it in their tommy box to bring home.

'A few years before the war my husband had been out of work for three and a half years and he was desperate to get a job. He and his friend used to go all over South Wales on their bicycles looking for work, but there was nothing about. He'd worked in Merthyr Vale and Plymouth colliery further up the valley but there was no work there for him anymore.

'In the end we went to London where he got a job and we stayed for eleven years, living there right through the blitz. When we returned he never went back down the mines. He took a job making toys in the Lines factory in Merthyr, which later became the Triang toy factory.'

Susie and Doris' lives centred around the village, partly because of lack of transport. 'In those days there was only the brake, like a horse and cart, if you wanted to go anywhere. There would be two rows of seats facing each other and a horse pulling us. I remember the first bus coming to Aberfan which caused great excitement and everybody came out to watch. It became a real treat if you could catch the bus up to Merthyr, but we couldn't afford it very often and if you didn't have the money you'd have to walk.'

The Barracks

Michael and Terry Donoghue

Michael was born at Pontygwaith in Aberfan. He tried to fight off attempts to send him underground, believing it wasn't fit work for a man. Similarly his son Terry was reluctant to join the pit, but was conscripted as a Bevin Boy and then found he loved the job. Michael Donoghue is believed to be the only miner from Merthyr Vale who went off to fight in the Spanish Civil War, this coming as no surprise to his family as he was known to have no respect for the mines. Terry, who's now 64, recalls his father's departure.

'I remember my father coming up to the bedroom the night before he went and telling me he had to go because he had to prove who the real communists were. He just came over to the bed and couched me up before he went. My mother obviously didn't want him to go and he wouldn't allow her to get me out of bed the following morning to see him off.

'My father was an incredible figure—a real adventurer. He always had a marvellous time and did exactly as he pleased. At fourteen he went underground in Merthyr Vale colliery but he was never going to get on for he just wasn't the sort to bow down to any management. In those days to do well you'd have to be given your own section of the pit, but he was militant from the day he started, always trying to encourage people to join the Federation and therefore wasn't liked by those that ran the pit and was unable to obtain his own patch.

'By the time he was sixteen he and his brother Humphrey joined the army, initially without the family knowing. He was sent to India but his mother found out where he was, reported the breach to the authorities and he was shipped home. It was back to the mines for him then. But he never liked mine working and eventually he was blacklisted from the pit because of his political activities. I remember for about 8 years no one would give him work because of his union activities and militancy. It was a terrible time because he was out of work for so long.

'At the time my mother had just eighteen shillings a week to feed the family of four—me, my sister and of course my father. I always remember her being worried about whether she'd be able to feed us and make ends meet. It's strange to think that we were better off when my father went off to fight in the Spanish Civil War for our dole money was suddenly replaced by more than £2 a week paid by the International Brigade.'

In 1936 when General Franco rose against the republican government in Spain, war broke out which was to last for three years. Unhappy with the British government's policy of non-intervention, a campaign was established to send arms, food and soldiers to Spain. Aid for Spain committees were set up all over the country, whilst the Miners Federation sought to persuade the government to change its mind and to send assistance. Thousands of anti-fascists from fifty different countries went to Spain to fight alongside the loyal Spaniards and formed the International Brigade together with its British battalion. Of the battalion's 170 Welsh volunteers, 116 were miners, about 25 per cent of whom were union officials. One in five was married and the average age was over 30.

The South Wales miners provided the largest regional group in the British battalion and many were killed. Even if they survived they faced problems on return, for the British government, following its non-intervention policy, introduced an act imposing up to two years imprisonment for International Brigade volunteers.

'The whole time he was there he only ever saw two tanks. But even when it was all over for the Welsh he didn't wait to be captured. He and seven others stowed away on a ship leaving Spain and hid in the chain locker, the area used to release the anchor. At first he was absolutely freezing and all he had to eat were scraps brought by a few seamen who were helping to hide him. In the end the captain found out but treated them well and allowed them off the ship in Scotland.

'My mother used to tell us how when he came walking back down the street on his return all he had to his name was what he stood up in—a shirt, pair of trousers and a pair of Spanish daps. He used to tell a story about how one of his friends was killed by a sniper. He waited without sleep for three days and two nights until he found the attacker and killed him.

'He then went off to Treforest, a few miles away from Merthyr Vale where he had the highly paid but dangerous job of cleaning the inside of the towers at the power station.

'During the Second World War he joined the navy. But for 18 months he avoided duty by volunteering to work in the mines. After my mother bought him everything to go back underground—clothes, a box and a jack—he went through the charade of turning up for duty, and then disappearing as he hated the thought of working underground. He was eventually caught out and had to work in the mines until he was again called up for the services. This time he gladly went.

'In the navy he was a first class stoker on HMS Norfolk which was hit during the battle with the Scharnhorst just off the coast of Russia. He survived but often told how some of his friends who were hurled into the sea lasted just two minutes in the cold water. He also used to tell of how he refused to salute the flag aboard ship and annoyed the captain when instead he stood in front of it whistling the Red Flag. His lanyard was stripped from him and he was thrown into clink for a day.

'He never returned to the pits after he was demobbed, but worked on construction sites as a steel fixer. My father had never wanted to be a miner and said it wasn't a fit job for a man and the pit wasn't a fit place to work because of all the dust.'

In 1943 Ernest Bevin, the Minister of Labour and National Service, gave men who were called up the option of entering the mines instead of joining the forces. However by midsummer only 3,000 men had so volunteered. Bevin then announced an extra 30,000 to 60,000 were needed by the end of the year and as a result one in every ten conscripts was sent underground, to become known as Bevin Boys. By the end of the war there were 45,000 such boys, and in 1948 there were still 20,000 completing their national service obligations. During the war anyone who had worked underground for more than three months wasn't allowed to leave without permission from the Ministry of Labour and this ring fence, as it became known, remained in force till 1950.

'In 1944 I was working as a garage hand and at 18 I was called up into the services. I had a medical for the navy but was told there was no vacancy and was then told to go to the army office just down the corridor. I was quite excited and looking forward to joining up but I was shocked when my papers eventually came through—I'd been conscripted into the mines as a Bevin Boy.

'My mother and father were very unhappy. It was a big shock for all of us when we discovered I had to go underground. I was so upset I refused to go into the pit— it's something I'd never dreamed of but eventually when I didn't turn up my father had to go to the court in Merthyr Tydfil on my behalf and he was warned I'd be jailed if I didn't go in.

'So my start in mining was very unhappy and very reluctant. I was sent off to train at Oakdale for four weeks and that was like a holiday camp. But when I got to Merthyr Vale it was all so different. I was eighteen years of age and I was classed underground as a boy. Even if you swore you'd receive a clout from one of the older miners. I was working as a collier's helper shovelling coal onto the conveyor—thank God conveyors had been installed by then.'

Despite his reluctant start Terry soon discovered he loved the work and never left the pits until he retired after a heart attack when he was 60. Although he didn't follow his father's political footsteps Terry was always a devoted socialist and moved on to work at Taff Merthyr colliery a few miles away where he was on the lodge NUM committee for thirty years, serving as chairman and vice-chairman.

He was born in 1926 and spent most of his early life in a terraced house in Victoria Street in Merthyr Vale. 'My childhood like most in Merthyr Vale during the thirties and early forties was extremely hard. I can remember coming home from school and my mother had just one egg in the house which my sister and I had to share for tea. My mother used to take in washing and go out to paper people's homes to try and earn a few extra shillings.

'But we were no worse off than others in the village. We were receiving just eighteen shillings from the dole, but there was a man living near us who had nine children and he was working in the pit bringing home just £2 a week.

'It was a happy time despite the hardship. People's front doors were always open and there was a very friendly atmosphere. But if you lived in Merthyr Vale you'd always be listening out to the hooter. If there was a bad fall underground or the mine owners simply had enough coal for their demands that week, they'd just send the men home. What would normally happen is that the men would work Monday, Tuesday and Wednesday and at the end of the third shift a hooter would sound. There was a special signal, so many hoots on the hooter, which told the men there'd be no more work for the rest of the week. It was really crafty because if you'd worked three days you couldn't claim the dole, but you'd still only be paid for the three days you'd worked.

'Those were the hardest times and it was then our families would have to turn to the parish asking for extra help. But the people who used to visit your house to assess your needs were really terrible. They were swines. I remember the case of somebody who had a piano that had been handed down from their mother when she died. When the parish found out, the family was ordered to sell it. A friend of my mother had to ask for help and when the parish officer came into the house and saw two statues of Venus over the fire, he told her to make sure they were covered up by the time of the next visit because they were rude. That was the type of power they held over your lives.'

Terry's wife Margaret also remembers visits from the parish to her home. 'We only had coconut mats on the floor but when they saw the sofa and a table and chairs around it, they told her she'd have to sell those first before she could claim help. My mother had the sense to say they belonged to her mother and we had to write to her really quickly before the parish checked out our story.'

Because Terry's father wasn't working he and his sister were given a free pair of shoes every year and his family was also given a voucher to have blankets from a store in Merthyr. He was also allowed free school dinners. 'I remember that the school didn't have any cutlery so we all had to take our own. We used to go off in the morning with a spoon tucked into our belts, like a gun in a cowboy's holster.

'At home everything we ate seemed to be a stew. My mother sent me to the corner shop with nine pence and strict instructions to get six pennies worth of meat pieces, usually scrag end of lamb and a penny's worth of parsnips and carrots mixed. That would make a stew big enough for an army and we had dough boys (dumplings) as big as my fist. We also had rabbit stew and even now I can't eat rabbit I had it so much as a kid. Liver and hearts were a real treat. But we never went hungry.'

That's more than can be said for his wife. 'I was then at the grammar school at Hengoed. I was entitled to free dinners but it was terrible because all those who had paid for their own dinners would be given a blue ticket whilst those having free ones would be given a white one. You stood out a mile and the girls made sure that only those with the same coloured ticket sat together. I remember someone asking if her friend could sit with her but because she had a white ticket she wasn't allowed to sit with those who had paid. In the end, although my mother never knew, I stopped going to have dinners in school. I would rather go hungry.'

She also didn't have the luxury of blankets from the parish. 'I used to share the bed with my two sisters. They slept up the top and me down the bottom, just like a tin of sardines. In winter we'd snuggle under my father's army coat and when the weather improved it would be put away in a big tin for the summer.'

'At Christmas my present was always a book. I must have read Little Women hundreds of times. All the girls I knew had a doll and I didn't. I'll never forget the Christmas morning when I came down and my father led me to the water boiler in the kitchen—he said Father Christmas had hidden a doll there for me. I cherished it for years.'

The colliery, Merthyr Vale, about 1890

34

The post-war crisis in the industry was most acute in South Wales. Manpower had fallen from 135,901 in 1937 to 107,624 in 1946 with output decreasing from 37,773,000 to 20,950,000 tons. Following the difficult years between 1918 and 1939, the government's wartime control and a critical need for coal in the post war years, nationalisation was seen as the realistic way forward. There was only token resistance from the mine owners and the coal industry was nationalised in 1947, just two years after the emergence of the National Union of Mineworkers.

The NUM and most miners hailed nationalisation as the beginning of a new era, but some were more pessimistic. Their fears were realised when the new minister for fuel and power, Hugh Gaitskill, announced that the brief honeymoon in the mining industry was over. There were thirty-four pit closures in South Wales up to 1950 as the NCB pursued a rationalisation policy of bigger production units.

In 1958 plans emerged for a major reorganisation at Merthyr Vale. At the time the pit employed 1,279 men and output had increased steadily since 1947 to 2,300 tons a day and the plans intended to increase production to 3,000 tons a day.

Prior to 1960 Merthyr Vale operated as two pits, the number one shaft mining the Four Feet seam, and the number two working the Five Feet Gellideg seam. The reorganisation which was completed in 1962 fully mechanised the pit, integrated the two operations and the number one pit was closed. Miners went underground via the number two pit although coal was still being brought to the surface from the number one entrance. The integration also included electrifying the winding gear and increasing underground conveyor capacity. Coupled with a new coal preparation plant and rail wagon loading facilities on the surface, the scheme allowed the pit to become one of South Wales' major coal producers right up to the disaster.

At a quarter past nine on 21 October 1966 people looked up into the sky as they heard a loud rumble. Some thought it was thunder and others that it was a low flying plane, for a belt of mist filled the lower part of the valley, preventing people from seeing the top of the mountainside.

As the tip moved down the mountainside it engulfed Pantglas junior school, two farm cottages and a number of houses. Within minutes 144 people, 116 of them children, were dead as part of the village was swamped by a sea of slurry and water.

Four days later parliament ordered an enquiry and a tribunal was established to ascertain the facts leading up to the disaster.

The initial tipping had taken place between the canal and the mountainside and it wasn't until the First World War that tipping began on the mountain to the west

The Disaster

of the canal. Here Tip 1 was mine rubbish discarded from the preparation plant and boiler, and reached to a height of 85 feet. Tip 2 was begun in 1918 and rose to 90 feet. Tip 3 was started in 1925 and reached 130 feet when Tip 4 took over in 1933. This rose to 147 feet, but it hadn't been added to since 1944 when a large part slipped down the mountainside. Tip 5 followed in 1945 and was used until 1956 when it was 171 feet high. Then the sixth tip was started in 1956, but additions to it were stopped in 1958 when complaints were received from a farmer that the tip material was spilling onto his land. This tip reached just 56 feet high.

Tip 7, the disaster tip, was started at Easter 1958 and was in use right up until the slip. It was the only one of the seven to contain tailings, the very fine particles left from the filtration plant after a chemical process has extracted all the coal. This plant had been completed in February 1962 and the tailings, according to the NCB, composed over 10 per cent of the tip but were concentrated lower down.

In mining terms slurry is defined as a mixture of coal and water, but the tip flow at Aberfan was widely described as such with the wet tailings becoming like quick-sand. This waste mixture had already trapped sheep on the mountain, and at one time a child who was pulled out leaving his gumboots sucked into the mess. In addition the valley was known for its high rainfall and there was a multitude of streams and springs on the slopes. Pantglas was often flooded, often to a depth of two feet six inches and once as deep as seven feet under the Black Bridge across the Aberfan road. Between 1952 and 1965 the area was severely flooded at least eleven times.

Merthyr Vale ward Labour Party regularly forwarded complaints to Merthyr Tydfil Borough Council who in turn had complained to the coal board about the slurry deposits since 1949, whilst a petition was sent from the school on behalf of parents. In 1963 the council even wrote to Mr. D.L. Roberts, the NCB's area mechanical engineer, expressing their concern over Tip 7 and pointing out the consequences if the tip slipped. The correspondance was never passed to the colliery manager.

But it wasn't just letters and petitions which should have alerted the NCB to the dangers. There were several examples in the past of tips sliding. Tip 4 at Aberfan had slipped down the hillside on 27 October 1944. Earlier, on 5 December 1939 some 180,000 tons of waste from Cilfnydd Common near Abercynon, five miles along the Merthyr to Cardiff road, slipped onto the road, crossed it and continued a further 720 feet on the far side, blocking the road to a depth of between 20 and 25 feet. It also filled a 540 feet length of the Glamorgan Canal, and blocked only a slightly shorter length of the railway.

Miners and railwaymen assembling at Paddington Station for a protest march against unemployment, 1963

However none of these events had led to a thorough investigation and tipping continued, piling unstable material ever higher and wider. As the streams around Tip 7 were covered its base became very wet, increasing the risk of a major slip.

At 7.30 on 21 October 1966, men going to work found that the top of the point of the tip had sunk by between nine and ten feet, and a track used for a crane had fallen in. Concerned, the crane-driver Gwyn Brown suggested to David Jones, a slinger, that he go down and report it to Leslie Davies, their charge-hand, who every Friday rendered his weekly report to the Unit Mechanical Engineer, Vivian Thomas. A messenger had to be sent as though there had been a telephone on top of the tip it had been removed because the wire connecting it with the mine had been repeatedly stolen, so David Jones set off down the mountainside. He made his report to Leslie Davies and advised him in turn to inform Vivian Thomas.

Vivian Thomas sent men with an oxy-acetylene burner to sever the overhanging rails and gave directions for the crane to be pulled back as far as possible. He also instructed Leslie Davies to stop tipping on Tip 7 and he himself would go up on the following Monday in order to organise tipping in a fresh place.

Leslie Davies, David Jones and the two men with the burning equipment arrived at the top about nine o'clock to find the tip had sunk another ten feet. Those below could not see what was starting to happen as the tip was still shrouded in mist.

The tip then started to move down the mountainside. Two farm cottages and their inhabitants were engulfed. It continued on across the disused canal and over the railway embankment where it destroyed the junior school and eighteen houses.

At the junior school one master and a whole class of thirty-four children died. The teacher was found with three children he had tried to save; the headmistress died in her study. A clerical worker died taking the dinner money, but her body shielded five children who miraculously survived. In all five teachers and 109 children from Pantglas junior school died.

At the senior school the headmaster was alerted when he saw houses between the schools had disappeared. He evacuated the school but as they prepared a roll call the water mains burst, bringing a further rush of water. Nobody brought out from under the tip after eleven o'clock was brought out alive.

The rescue operation was joined by police and civil defence workers. At 10.30 the BBC carried a newsflash which prompted a stream of help. The army, navy and the miners from Merthyr Vale all joined in, working through the night to dig the graves, and helping to evacuate a further 60 people from nearby houses.

Bethania Chapel was set up as a mortuary and preparations started for the mass funeral for 81 of the children and one adult, a mother to be buried with her two children. A giant floral cross measuring 130 feet with arms 40 feet wide was created at the cemetery.

Dignitaries soon arrived to see the horror for themselves and offer what support they could. Amongst them were the Prime Minister, Harold Wilson; Lord Snowden; the Duke of Edinburgh and the Secretary of State for Wales. The Queen visited the village after the funeral, laid a wreath, met bereaved parents and had tea with a local councillor who had lost seven relatives.

On the evening of the disaster an appeal was started to raise money to relieve the hardship and rehabillitate the village. The fund closed in January 1967, but money kept pouring in from over forty countries and eventually totalled £1,750,000.

The fund paid for holidays, whilst Princess Margaret launched a toy appeal to which the response was so great that four disused buildings were needed by the post office in Cardiff to temporarily house them all.

The tribunal itself was set up on 25 October under the chairmanship of Lord Justice Edmund Davies. A preliminary meeting was held on 8 November and after starting its proceedings three weeks later, it heard evidence and deliberated for 76 days, setting a new record for the longest sitting tribunal in British history. It met initially in Merthyr and subsequently in Cardiff.

Lord Robens, chairman of the NCB, gave evidence to say that no-one could have known there was a spring under the mountain. Indeed the NCB persistently denied responsibility, blaming 'a coincidence of a set of geological factors'. However the report, published in August 1967, clearly placed the blame on the board, scathingly refuting their allegation that the disaster could not have been forseen.

The report spoke of 'not wickedness but of ignorance, ineptitude and a failure of communications.' The board had to concede that the disaster stemmed from their failure to initiate any policy in relation to the siting, control, inspection and management of tips. In the words of Philip Wein, the board's Q.C. at the tribunal 'Blame for the disaster must rest upon the National Coal Board. Responsibility begins with management. Clear instructions were not given. Nor was any procedure laid down so that both officials and workmen were left without proper guidance.'

Gaynor Madgewick

Gaynor Madgewick has only spent one year of her life away from Aberfan. For a brief time she lived in a village a few miles away, but hated it and returned home, though with the pit's closure she's again starting to think of moving.

For Gaynor, then Gaynor Minett, it was an ordinary Friday. As usual her brother Carl, a year younger than her, complained that he did not want to go to school and pleaded with his mother to let him stay at home. She coaxed him into going to lessons, reminding him it was the last day of the week with the lure of the weekend ahead.

On the way into school Gaynor bought sweets from the little tuck shop on the nearby banking, and then joined the rest of the school in assembly. The village was soon alive with the sound of the children singing All Things Bright and Beautiful, a favourite assembly hymn.

Afterwards Gaynor went into the classroom taking her seat at the back of the class alongside one of her best friends, Paul Davies. The teacher, Mr. Davies, then took out the blackboard and set the class some maths exercises. As the children sat silently carrying out their work, Gaynor remembers a sound that was to haunt her for the rest of her life.

'We could hear a terrible terrible sound, a rumbling sound—it was so loud. It seemed as if the school went dead, you could hear a pin drop, and I was suddenly petrified. The whole school went numb. Everybody was glued to their seats they were so frightened. Something told me to get up from my seat and run. I managed to get up and ran to the end of my desk—I could see the black outside, and the noise was getting louder and louder.'

As the sea of black slag then engulfed her class and everything in it, Gaynor was pushed to the back wall of the classroom and was for a while knocked unconscious. When she awoke the full horror of what had happened was quite impossible for an eight year old to comprehend.

The boy who had sat alongisde Gaynor was later found to have died, as was her teacher, along with dozens of other children who were not only her classmates but the children with whom she had grown up. Her friend Dawn Andrews limped out of the debris and climbed through the roof that had collapsed. Gaynor remembers shouting to her to run for help and as one of the first to get out of the school, she ran to tell bewildered villagers that the school had fallen down.

For four years Gaynor hardly mentioned the disaster, speaking briefly only to her parents and doctors who had the job of trying to untangle the terrible psychological terrors locked in the childrens' minds. But four years later, sitting at her desk in her new school, she was suddenly compelled to recall the events of the day that changed Aberfan for ever. She snatched up a little blue exercise book and started frantically to write—hardly stopping until her story was told.

On the cover of the book she wrote My True Life Story, A Sad Story, ironically even stopping to fill in her form name and number on the cover of the text book.

The words she then went on to write, retelling a nightmare that no one could ever have described better, shook psychiatrists and made those who saw it cry all over again. With blood trickling down her face and a fear that her leg had been torn off and carried away with the moving sea of waste, she came around to face the appalling scene of the classroom.

'I woke to find a horrible nightmare just about to begin in front of my eyes. ... Bodies lay crushed and buried, and the survivors lay looking at their best friends dead. I can just see someone's hand through the crack in the wall. I didn't know whether it was a boy or girl. I squeezed the hand and pinched it to see if it was alive but I could see that it was dead. It was a terrible nightmare coming true. Next to me on my right was David Bates. He had cut his head open and his face was blood red. I picked up a book and it was called Through the Garden Gate and that too was drenched in blood, but I lay there reading it. I was too dazed and shocked to scream or to do anything but I lay there reading this book while others were petrified and screaming for help. Everything in the school was dead and we all now started getting worried as no help had come. I really thought we'd all die. The muck was at least a yard and a half up the wall. Windows were smashed and nothing was left whole. It was a sigh of relief as a man's face stood looking at us through the window. I could guess he was thinking "Where to start first". There were so many of us trapped and it took a long time to rescue us all. ... He hauled dead bodies through the window and my friend who was cut. I can see my Grandpa in the window. As he looked around with tears in his eyes I called to him and he saw me. It was then I started to cry as I reached out my arms for him but he couldn't come for me as there were so many bodies in the way. It was a terrible feeling to wait for someone to rescue you.'

It actually took her grandfather Stan Richards a quarter of an hour to reach her and he was faced with the agonizing task of having to rescue other children whose bodies lay in the way of his granddaughter. Gaynor now recalls 'He didn't know what to do. He struggled to rescue other children before me, but at least all the ones he carried out were alive. First he had to untrap my hand and then he carried me out. From there I was passed from man to man and then taken away in an ambulance.' In fact it took four men to free Gaynor and she was eventually passed to her grandmother who stood sobbing in the muck with Gaynor's parents.

As Gaynor was passed safe but seriously injured into the ambulance she didn't realise that still trapped inside and probably already dead were her brother and sister. But she does remember how she looked back at the carnage as she was carried away, suddenly realising that the torn little bodies that lay behind her were those of her dead friends and as she was carried out amongst other screaming children, she realised even then that it was the last time she would see many of them.

While she was in hospital during those early days the enormity of the disaster was slowly brought home to her. Her book recalls 'The day went past with casualties pouring in, but none badly hurt, just the one or two. The night came when the parents came in and they all looked so pale and their eyes red with weeping. My mother sat down and my father, also with him was my grandma. My father talked to me I felt so hurt to see them so helpless. I asked my father whether Carl and Marilyn were all right. He replied in a toned voice "they were gone", I just couldn't believe it. I didn't cry but just hugged my father feeling so weak as I'd never see them again. The following day in the afternoon I had kept awake dreaming of what had happened and suddenly I broke down. I sobbed and tears trickled down my face, tears of death. The doctor, Gordon, came to me and asked me what was wrong. I told him and he hugged me and the expression on his face was so sad. I sobbed on his shoulder and I can just see his face. He lay me down and gave me a sedative and told me they were gone to heaven and they'd be loved there as God took care of them. I quietened down and shut my eyes. His hand went through my hair, his feelings for my sorrow was there in his heart too.'

Gaynor and her best friend Susan Maybanks soon realised how serious the disaster had been, as they were allowed to watch and listen to television and radio reports throughout the day.

Gaynor was one of the most seriously hurt of the survivors, and stayed in hospital suffering from leg and hip injuries. On Christmas Eve she was finally allowed home. But her scars, both physical and mental took many months to heal, and it was some time before she started to lead anything like a normal life again. A few days after she returned home her father took her in her wheelchair to the cemetery not far from her home to visit the graves where her brother and sister had been buried

The Price of Coal

The agony of someone's heart
Is all for the price of coal,
The death of miners, hunger and
    strikes,
Are all for the price of coal.

But worse still there is another thing
Just for the price of coal.
The death of one hundred children and
    more
Was all for the price of coal.

Is that what we pay for the fire in the
    grate?
Anger, pain and even hate?
Is this the price of coal?
                Ruth Mars, Treorchy, Rhondda

Tender Little Children

In the dark Welsh valley,
On the mountainside,
Lay the little children
Close to where they died.
Their little lives are ended
Before they reach their goal,
Tender little children
Have paid the price for coal.
                April Oldman, Deal, Kent

Poems taken from Aberfan: A memorial written by children, compiled by Margery Chadwick Harris while she had lain helpless in hospital. That day, although painful, was something of a turning point and she started to come to terms with what had happened.

Later she was able to start walking again and remembers that she had a lot of money and was invited to parties frequently. Slowly she started to go back onto the streets to play with her friends, but was always struck by the fact that most of her old pals were missing. It wasn't until two years later when she was ten that she made new friends, older than the ones she had lost.

The disaster not only shaped Gaynor's life, but changed the future of a quiet valley village whose name would only have been known to a few if the disaster had never happened.

She believes that those who survived the disaster have had their lives completely changed. 'It gives you a respect for living. You're thankful just to be here and all my friends seem to be very placid, I never argue with people. We seem to be different, for I never discuss the disaster with friends—I think you do tend to wipe it out.'

She still thinks constantly about what her brother and sister would have been like and what they'd have been doing now. Her father, long after his only son's death, had painted in yellow on the ladder he used for his builders' business the words H.C. Minett and son.

Gaynor also feels that her generation have lost a great deal. Most of them found it difficult to go back to school and when they did, they were constantly being interviewed and could not concentrate on leading a normal life. She believes that most of them missed out totally on education, and children who would have gone on to good jobs and further education were robbed of the chance.

She doesn't know anyone in her year who went on to university or further education and says as a result the pit that had so altered their lives was the only door open to most men who then went underground. A few others went into factories. 'We were a generation that lost out. We lost out on our education and on our futures. I can't think of any of us who ever did really well and most of us just stayed and grew up in the village. We haven't gone far at all.'

The last words of her book show her depth of feeling. 'I hope in four to five years time I will have the honour of giving birth to my children and I couldn't care how much pain I go through as no pain can hurt as much as the past. That's one pain that will never be forgotten. The agonising torture of death and sorrow which will dwell through the World for ever and torture minds of the lonely citizens of the little village of Aberfan, a name that will never be forgotten.

Gaynor is now divorced and has three children of her own. Every day she faces a constant reminder of the tragedy as she lives directly opposite the pit gates. But she says she feels no bitterness towards the pit and the waste it produced which caused the disaster. 'Although I feel angry that not enough was done about the tips, I don't feel bitter about it. I grew up with slag heaps and it gave work to hundreds of men for all those years. My father worked there until he retired early because of the dust, and set up his own business.

'But what I can't accept is what some people believe, that it was an act of God. Some people say that things always happen for a reason, but I don't believe that. My mother used to be an atheist, but she now believes and is comforted by the thought that the two children she lost have gone to heaven.

'I always believed in God, but I kept on asking myself why I hadn't died and I blamed myself for allowing my brother and sister to die.'

Gaynor has already told her oldest son James about the disaster. Although she has never allowed him to read the book she wrote when she was twelve, she plans to give it to him when he's older. 'I'd like all my children to know what happened. I think they should be thankful for their own lives and know the true meaning of life.'

'Where people have got the courage from all these years to go on with life I don't know. But I do know that the fact I survived and have gone on to have my own children has made me proud of myself.'

Army of diggers attacks the buried school

Left: A house crushed by the tip Right: Inside the school

45

Left: PC Victor Jones carrys Susan Maybanks to safety   Right: The children's communal grave

Jessie Meredith

Jessie used to work at the Hoover factory in Cambuslang in Scotland and was sent to Merthyr on a training course. She knew about mining and its difficulties for her father had been a Scottish miner and died as a result of silicosis. On the course she met her future husband David, who was soon in turn sent on a course to Cambuslang. There he stayed and married Jessie in 1950. They constantly visited Aberfan before making it their home in 1962. Just four years later the disaster was to rob them of their only daughter, and for many years afterwards Jessie was afraid of the rain.

'I was afraid to go out if it rained. If it rained in the night I would spend hours by the window looking out watching in case the water came down to the houses again. I was afraid of the water and I used to say to my boy "if it rains heavily get your gran up to the mountain. Don't worry about the house, let it run away."'

The fund set up after the disaster helped pay for Jessie and other families from the village to go on a holiday to Jersey. Even there the fear couldn't be erased from her mind. 'I used to phone home and ask if it was still raining in Aberfan. While the tip was still there I was afraid we had not seen the end of it and I was worried that if it rained heavily again I wouldn't be there to look after everybody.'

For Jessie it has never really stopped raining since that October day in 1966 when she first looked out of her window and saw a light drizzle coming down. Only now after twenty-five years is that fear subsiding and at last the awful knot of anxiety that would take hold of her is beginning to unfurl.

It had been a normal day in the Meredith household just a few hundred yards away from the school. 'Suzanne as always had made her way up to her friend Angela's house in the morning. She was wearing a tartan skirt and a little jumper. I had started by cleaning up the house and then had gone to the corner shop just a few doors away to get a few things, when I thought to myself about how the street used to get flooded. As I was in the shop there was dirty black water coming down the hill, and as I was waiting my turn to be served I shouted out that we were going to be flooded. As I dashed back to the house with my little baby Alan, who was just one, in my arms, I fell over the milk bottles.

'With that my friend Glenys from a few doors away arrived with her daughter Sian who was dirty. She said Sian had come home from class all covered in dirt, and she had thrust her into my arms before running back up to the school. I asked Sian what had happened and she said the school had fallen down.

'I didn't know what to do, so I went around to Glenys' house where the door was wide open and a stream of dirty water was just rushing through.

'I ran up to the top then and when I saw that the school had fallen down, my legs just turned to jelly. I couldn't walk. I just stood there dazed as all the time water flooded my home. Glenys came past and said she hadn't seen Suzanne.'

Jessie was to wait at the school for an agonizing ten hours not having had a sign of, or word about her daughter. As the men dug around her she stood and waited for news. At about 7 o'clock that night she was told to go to the Bethania Chapel. Even then, despite her worst fears, she believed Suzanne was still alive, right up to the moment she was told that she could go inside to see her dead child.

'Up until then I had hoped that the chapel was a hospital, but as I went into Bethania people were coming out who had been told their children had gone. Until I went in I still had that hope that they were just lost. When I went in all the pews were covered with little blankets and under them lay the little children. They picked up the blankets and showed me every girl until I came to Suzanne and said she was mine. There wasn't a mark on her except a little scratch over her mouth, even her clothes were clean.

'What I missed most was the noise and fun around the house. Suzanne was boisterous and full of fun. Our house was as quiet as a mouse after she'd gone.'

Jessie never blamed the colliery or people who had been working on the pit. 'I went to the top of the tip soon after to see what had happened for myself. You would never have dreamed that those men could have known that would happen or that they would have let it happen. It wasn't their fault and I never blamed them.'

'But even now, twenty-five years later, I still try to puzzle it out ... why, why, why ... and I still can't find the answer. It's even hard to believe it was twenty-five years ago, it seems like twenty-five days, for there's hardly a day goes by when I don't think of something about the disaster. I think about what Suzanne would be doing now if she was still alive. Would she be married? Would she have children?'

Jessie believes that time has helped heal the wounds of Aberfan. 'We're getting back to normal. There was a time when that's all we talked about, but now that doesn't happen very often. The mothers used to get together to share their grief and their feelings, but that doesn't happen any more. But the disaster has left a huge gap in Aberfan. We've lost a generation.'

Only now can Jessie face the rain without the fear that used to grip her and only now can she finally stop asking 'Is it still raining in Aberfan?'

The search continues amongst wrecked houses

Dr. Arthur Jones

Arthur Jones came from a strict Welsh background. His father, from Tywyn in Gwynedd, was a research physicist living in Teddington, Middlesex, but only Welsh was allowed to be spoken in the home and only Welsh maids employed. He remembers seeing Welsh miners looking for work in England, only owning the clothes they stood up in. In 1952, as a quaili-fied doctor, Dr. Jones came to Aberfan to live and practise, both of which he's still doing.

'It was as if it was all predestined that the mission I had always known I was to carry out was waiting at Aberfan.'

The morning of the disaster Dr. Jones should have been at his local surgery. However he'd been pestered the day before by a family over the condition of a patient and fearing they were going to continue to disrupt him in the morning, he decided not to go into the surgery early and to do some work at home.

At 9.25 he had a call from a nurse to say that a wall had collapsed at the school. He rang up a local chemist and asked him to have ready his stock of dangerous and strong drugs which he knew he would need for serious injuries.

'I thought there would be heavy casualties but obviously did not have any idea of how bad it was going to be until I arrived.'

He was the first doctor on the scene and found rescuers already at work. 'I remember stopping those who were trying to dig out the dinner lady. I just had this inbred fear that by disturbing the slurry around her, they could bring more slurry down on others. We worked on and on until we had got the last living child out. Then the battalions arrived.'

All he could do for the children still living was to give them injections for the pain and send them straight to hospital, many more were past his help. His work at the scene was minor compared to what was to come in the next few years.

'My work afterwards was more like that of a pastor. People had to face not only grief but bitterness, anger and even guilt. The first real thing that happened were the terrible nightmares people suffered, reliving the event time and time again. That went on for months. There was a terrible worry and pressure on people while the tip was still there, and every time there was a row over what was to be done about the tip my surgery would be full the next day. The stress and anxiety trig-gered off by what to do would affect people's health.

'It was predicted at the time that a lot of people might suffer from heart attacks brought on by the stress and grief, but that didn't happen. Other experts predicted that there would be a number of suicides, but that didn't happen either. These people hadn't allowed for the resilience of the families involved. It was psychological problems that hit worst.

'One thing that did happen within a short time afterwards was that the birth rate went up. Also many people were drinking a lot more and for some time after I had to deal with people who had serious drink problems, and for people who already had health problems, those problems increased.

'From the time of the disaster for about the following six years I dealt with people who suffered break downs. There was no set pattern or any time when it could be expected to happen. It happened at different times for different people.

'After the disaster I warned that the community would have to come to accept its guilt. This guilt came out in many ways. There were the so-called guilty men who were blamed for what happened; they suffered themselves and were the victims of a hate campaign. But it wasn't only them. Women who had sent their children who hadn't wanted to go to school that day suffered terrible feelings of guilt.

'Again, that particular morning a young boy had been brought to the surgery to see me. Because I hadn't arrived he was kept at the surgery and did not make it to school and survived because of that strange set of coincidences. Soon after the disaster he had to have a policeman to escort him to school because of threats to him from people in the village. There were people sending his family abusive letters because they felt he should have died like the rest of the children. Grief and guilt came out in many different ways. There was a strange bitterness between families who had lost children and those who hadn't; people just could not help it.'

Dr. Jones recalls it was even difficult for people whose children died after the disaster from unrelated causes. He remembers the case of one small child who didn't go to the school hit by the disaster. A few months later she died from pneumonia and although her family were bereaved and grieving he says they felt they should not be grieving like the other parents.

However he thinks that time has finally laid the guilt to rest. 'When I look out of my surgery window now it's strange that the winding gear I'd always seen has gone. I think most of the problems from Aberfan are over now. A lot of people thought because of what had happened at Aberfan it would be the last pit to close, but I think most at the end were glad to see it go.'

Mike Meredith

When the disaster happened Mike Meredith was the recently appointed Welsh affairs reporter on the NCB's in-house newspaper. He was sitting in the press office in Cardiff when the first call came in from a reporter on the South Wales Echo, the area's evening paper.

'The reporter spoke to Islwyn Evans who was then public relations officer but at first he simply refused to believe that such a tragedy could have happened. I made a few calls and soon realised it was every bit as bad as the reporter had said.'

Mike, who later became the board's press officer, called his London based news-desk who ignored his concern and told him to carry on with plans to visit Swansea to carry out a routine interview. Only later that day did they realise their mistake and send him to Aberfan, where he arrived about 8 o'clock that evening.

'The thing that struck me when I went on a visit to the colliery manager's office was that it was festooned with certificates for safety, but absolutely no heed was paid to the tips and there was no legislation covering the way tips were built up. At the time the valleys were in an appalling mess with pit heaps discarded everywhere. But after Aberfan the action was feverish and an examination of every one of the tips in South Wales was ordered covering the 540 tips in the National Coal Board's hands and probably an equal number which were privately owned, even though the board inherited 500 million tons of waste when the industry was nationalised.

'Nobody had previously thought about the tips at all and since mining began in the 1700's waste was simply dumped anywhere the steep sided valleys allowed. As a result of the examination, 30 of the tips in South Wales were found to be unsafe and had to be tended to immediately. Those tips were removed within three years.

'For eighteen months after the disaster people were really frightened. Whenever it rained our civil engineering department would be overwhelmed with calls, and a special department was set up to look just at the safety of tipping.

'Since Aberfan £60 million has been spent on tip removal and contouring. But despite the warnings and the work, within years a problem developed at Lewis Merthyr colliery just a few miles away when a terrible storm sent water and debris dashing down onto houses underneath and several homes were affected.

'After that the NCB further improved their drainage systems and designed all tips on a computer with the angle of repose being carefully considered and planned to survive storms of once in a hundred years' intensity. We now lead the world in tip technology.'

View of the tip slide onto Aberfan

52

Graham Schewitz

Graham Schewitz came from a Cardiff sea-faring family and joined the merchant navy, leaving in 1954. He became a trainee miner in the same year, working at Abercynon colliery, spending seven years studying for his diploma in mining at the Polytechnic of Wales. He became undermanager at Abercynon in 1962, when aged 32, and two years later manager at Trelewis Drift. After the disaster he was moved to Merthyr Vale and given the task of trying to restore good morale and the pit to profitability, as losses had reached £195,000 per annum.

'Where men had lost so many of their own close relations morale was at rock bottom and there were only two places to go. We either shut the pit or worked to build it back up again. We had to reinstate the heart of the pit.' At the time the men were on a day wage system paying seventy-eight shillings and one penny a day. 'Obviously some were paid more, others less. But with no bonus scheme or productivity incentive it was difficult to boost production and the only option lay in overtime and in boosting the men's morale. Savings were made by offering voluntary redundancy with enhanced payments to the older miners, and the workforce was reduced to 765. By the following year production was back up to 308,000 tons a year, and the colliery was making a profit of £222,000.

'The pit became not only profitable and productive but also a happy place. At times it was just one long laugh. During the time I worked there, there was a great local pride and loyalty for the pit. Three-quarters of the miners lived within a few miles of the pit between Troedyrhiw and Aberfan.'

Because of the disaster the pit also received many visitors. 'One visit in December 1967, from the chairman of the board Alf Robens, may have even changed things for every miner in Britain. Before Aberfan important visitors had only ever seen the clean side of mining. I think when Robens visited the pit during the disaster he was quite shocked, and he returned the following December. I remember feeling relieved there was snow on the ground so he couldn't see everything.

'At the time we were using hydraulic prop supports at the face and I asked him for power supports which are safer to use and a great help to production. Soon after we were given them for two faces. But I think most would remember his visit for a completely different reason.

'When he approached the NUM lodge secretary, Bill King, Bill in his usual fashion asked him if it was fair that a man should work on New Year's Day. Robens replied that he didn't, and Bill said that the miners had to. I'm sure it's no coincidence that the following year miners throughout Britain were given the day off.

'A few years later he returned to the pit when I asked for investment in the coal washery. That was granted and the investment enabled us to introduce a dual market policy. Before that we were just supplying coal for the phurnacite works in the Cynon valley where smokeless fuel was being made for the rest of the country. Now we were able, thanks to the new investment, to mix the duff or reject coal so that it was acceptable for use at Aberthaw power station.'

In the late 60's Graham continued to try to boost morale, this time by organising a series of teach-ins at the local social club. Each week was given over to a different theme complete with a campaign name. Posters were displayed throughout the pit to try to encourage the men to attend. ITMA, named after the war time comedy of Tommy Handley 'It's that man again', was one of the first. 'ITMA was the nickname given to the under manager John Waters. He was a bit of a tiger and would go storming about the pit until everyone would say "It's that man again."'

Another week was called flower power week when psychedelic posters appeared all over the pit to try to lure men to the meeting. 'The aim was to get them all together to talk about how we could increase production, but mainly to get us all together as a team.' The men were paid fifteen shillings each, the price of a few pints, to turn up and entertainment including a pianist would be thrown in. It's little wonder that often as many as 300 men would arrive for the meetings.

In the mid 70's the pit received another important visit and again Bill King was instrumental in what was to be achieved. He'd had a chance meeting with the then NCB chairman Derek Ezra after gate-crashing a party thrown by the board during the NUM's conference week, and talked about the problems at Merthyr Vale.

Six days later Merthyr Vale's alarmed manager had a telephone call to say Ezra had decided to make a visit, which left him with the huge problem about how to wine and dine him. The men knew it was important to create the right image if they were to obtain any new investment for the pit, but the only place they had to eat was the none too clean pit canteen used by workers from throughout the pit.

'I'd visited large pits in Staffordshire where the Board had used the ladies' rest-room to set up a separate VIP dining area in the staff canteen and decided to try to create our own.' But the Board would not pay a penny towards the scheme as the general policy was that all the men should eat in the same place, so other methods had to be used. Graham, who was known as a heavy smoker, had already obtained a

Some of the miners at Merthyr Vale as recalled by Graham Schewitz.

Danny Cold Blood
Billy Odd Coppers
Dilwyn Hook and Eye
Will One Song
Georgie Pub
Dai Fat
Dai Sweat
Johnny Howler
Tommy Tinker
Trevor Bung-guts
Eddie Dixie
Billy One Eye
George Aberdare
Gwylim Gas Oven
Gwylim Tablets
Bill Bee Hive
Billy Iron Boot
Ianto Aye Aye
Willy Want
Jack the Black
Freddie Greenfly
Dai Shake hands
Dai Little Engine
Will Cup Final
Tommy Tin Hat
Tommy Duck Egg
Tommy Dunkirk
Will Bumble
Tommy Cocoa
Dai Gold Watch
Danny Jumping Bean
Glyn Oily Evans
Dai Lots of Kids Davies

bowling kit and bag by sending Embassy cigarette vouchers away for free gifts. As he thumbed through the catalogue one day he saw crystal glasses on offer and had a brainwave. Instructions went out to the engineers to smoke as many Embassy cigarettes as possible, and to make sure they handed in the vouchers.

But it didn't stop there. He saw a smart new dinner service in the Green Shield catalogue and miners were light-heartedly put under orders to save as many as possible. Even face workers couldn't escape from the drive to make Ezra's visit one never to forget, for the women in the pit canteen discovered that the Bowyers meat pie firm was offering a free set of cutlery in exchange for a large number of their pie wrappings. Although the women's cooking was highly praised, so much so that people who didn't work in the pit were known to go to the canteen to eat, pies were suddenly prominent on the menu every day.

'When Derek Ezra arrived at the pit both he and the area manager, Phillip Weekes, looked around in amazement at the apparent splendour. Realising that they might think the pit's budget had been misused, I told them what we'd done to add a touch of class to the colliery. It was all very funny.'

Ezra listened for hours to the problems and was told not only that they needed new machinery, but that investment was required to break through a solid wall of rock called the Church Fault between Merthyr Vale and Bedlinog which was stopping the men from getting to massive coal reserves.

'There was a bit of disagreement between us over the man rider. I told Ezra that the men had a man rider to bring them out and that was enough. It carried them up a slope coming out and I said that I didn't think it was too much to ask for the men to walk in to work. In fact I remember saying that in future the men would bless me for not having heart attacks because of the exercise they were taking. I'd forgotten Ezra had recently suffered heart problems himself and he was quite adamant that the men should have a man rider taking them into work.'

Ezra dealt quickly with the issues. A man rider was installed and contractors hired to open up the Merthyr Church fault. In addition he nominated the pit for an environmental award after seeing how it had been cleaned up in a year in which the coalfield had launched a campaign for tidy pit surfaces. It won not just an NCB award, but also a certificate of commendation from the European Architectural Year Business and Industry panel.

Bob Bad Luck
George no.8 Jones
Alan Jones Swansea Road
Alan Jones Merthyr Vale
Dai Wireless
Bomper Jackson
Dai the Lamproom
Dai Bothers
Dai Electric
Lone Lanto
Chippy Williams
Dai the Hole Davies
Jack Coventry Williams
Euchin Cute
Dai Stonedust
Brian Gonzo Davies
Cyril Jones Spanny
Will Thomas Dogs
Slogger Carpenter
Joe Dagie Davies
Dickie Drunk
Dai Pipe
Dai Left Wing
Tommy Rats
Cocker Nash
Jeff Jaffa Roberts
Blondie Morgan
Billie Bungem
Totty Watkins
Harold Nye Davies
Colin Sooty Davies
Dickie Bach
Bill Captain Birds Eye Gerard
Alan Poisoned Dwarf Walters
Cyril Silent Night George

Some members of Merthyr Vale colliery NUM lodge, 1984

After a strike in January and February 1972 which was settled by the Wilberforce Inquiry's independent recommendations, the miners became the highest paid workers in the industrial league. By 1974 they had slipped to eighteenth place and decided to reclaim what they saw as their rightful position. Negotiations failed and a four week strike started on 9 February 1974 which resulted in Edward Heath's Conservative government announcing a state of emergency, a three day week and a general election for 28 February. The return of a minority Labour government resulted in an early settlement.

The agreed return to work terms included a new scheme for sufferers from pneumonoconiosis and as Merthyr Vale had always had a high percentage of dust cases, indeed it was so bad the pit was referred to as The Black Hole of Calcutta, the pit was used to establish the levels of compensation the men would be paid.

After the problems of the early 70's, the later years were to prove a time of great investment at Merthyr Vale. In May 1974 the NCB replaced the last two steam locomotives which had been used to shunt wagons on the pit surface with diesels. But at the same time the board warned that all pits would have to stand on their own feet and generate profits to provide capital for future investment.

Whilst productivity in the area reached 29.8 hundredweight per manshift, the results at Merthyr Vale were outstanding and the pit was praised for reaching a new productivity record of 51.2 hundredweight.

At the time the pit had two power loading coalfaces in the seven feet seam, one of which was equipped with a new automatic stower for building roadside packs. This utilised waste materials from roadway rippings cutting out the need to form a support with timber or concrete blocks. It was on trial for the first time in Wales and proved to be such a success in saving manpower, time and materials that the board announced it would introduce the system into other pits in the area.

However from 1975 some miners believe things started to look quite bleak as mining became more difficult. Coal was harder to reach and more geological problems were encountered. At one time, because of a dispute at the Taff Merthyr colliery a few miles away, water was being pumped into old districts lying to the side. This caused problems for Merthyr Vale as water collected in the limestone of the valley and percolated into the colliery causing some areas to become waterlogged. The problems had a parallel in the management for from the retirement of Graham Schewitz in 1975 to the pit's closure in 1989 it had seven different managers.

The 1984/85 strike

During this time a number of schemes were mooted suggesting the merger of Merthyr Vale with other pits nearby. The biggest merger plan came in January 1975, on the same day that the board announced it was closing Ogilvie colliery in the Rhymney valley. The plan envisaged investing a further £4,500,000 to integrate the pit with two of the other largest collieries in South Wales—Deep Navigation and Taff Merthyr, so allowing the combined pits to reach an output of 1,000,000 tons of coal a year. The Board estimated the three pits' total reserves at around 25 million tons, enough to probably secure output into the next century.

But the integration did not proceed. Each time the idea was raised they could never convince the NUM of any financial or mining advantages. At the time the pit was losing skilled miners to the Hoover washing machine plant at Merthyr which was providing clean and highly paid jobs and the union was worried that a merger would lead to a reduction in morale and a mass exodus to Hoover. They were also concerned about the future of a large number of apprentices for there would have been definite job cuts. In addition each pit would have lost its identity and the three NUM lodges would have faced integration.

Despite the rejection of this scheme the next few years were to see great investment and big developments at Merthyr Vale. In 1976 production started on a brand new £500,000 B20 coal face, which at the time was the biggest, most sophisticated, and most productive unit ever launched in a Welsh mine. In less than a month productivity soared to 236 hundredweights per manshift. Over 200 roof supports each costing £1,000 were installed along the face length and an automatic detector system for the deadly methane was installed.

Underground fans were added in 1976 and 1977 as part of another major investment programme to facilitate the extraction of methane which could otherwise collect in areas away from the ventillation system. The fans had to be run seven days a week, twenty-four hours a day, but their extraction site some 800 yards down the colliery created a warm damp atmosphere. Here crickets, which fed on orange peel, apple cores and crumbs left behind by the men, found a tremendous nesting place.

The noise they created was deafening and many miners whose fathers and grandfathers before them had sunk the pit and brought it to success grew afraid of the crickets, many refusing to go near the area where they nested. After complaints from the men, the NCB's vermin officer was brought in to try to exterminate them, but he never completely succeeded. Many men would continue to dash through the area fearing they'd take crickets home with them on their clothes.

Bill 'Captain Birds Eye' Gerard, under-manager Merthyr Vale, 1972

In 1979 a further investment programme costing £2.1 million was launched to extend the life of Merthyr Vale by up to twenty years. The aim was to open up new reserves lying behind the underground Church Fault, to develop three new coal faces and to further improve manriding facilities.

At that time there were 621 miners at the pit and the workings spread over an area covering four square miles concentrated on a seven feet seam which supplied top quality dry steam coal for the manufacture of smokeless fuel. The deepest workings lay 775 metres underground. There were more than ten miles of underground railways and around three miles of high speed belt conveyors in daily use. There were estimated workable coal reserves of 7.1 million tonnes.

Despite the euphoria caused by all this investment there were ominous signs of impending doom, possibly beginning in the 1950's when cheap oil was imported from the Middle East. There were around 50 to 60 pits in South Wales at the time but closures had already begun as the government began to switch its energy requirements from coal to oil. There was a respite when the Arab-Israeli wars in the 1960's sent oil prices soaring, accompanied by fears that oil prices could continue to rise through the 70's and 80's because of instability in the Middle East. So the 1974-79 Labour government announced its Plan for Coal which aimed for 120 million tonnes output by 1985.

But Labour lost the 1979 election and in October the same year a leaked cabinet minute from the new Conservative government stated that 'a nuclear programme would have the advantage of removing a substantial portion of electricity from disruption by industrial action of coal miners and transport workers.' In December the Tories announced an intention to build one nuclear power station a year from 1982 for the next ten years. At the same time British Steel revealed it was increasing imports of coking coal to one fifth in 1979/80 and to one half in 1980/81.

In 1980 the government declared that by 1983-84 all operating grants given to the NCB would be ended. From then on the board would have to make a profit.

After the Conservatives had been re-elected in 1983, they announced that 65,000 jobs would have to be shed from the coal industry if it was to break even by 1987/88. Ian McGregor, who as chief executive of British Steel had axed 85,000 jobs between 1980 and 1983, was appointed chairman of the NCB in September 1983.

On 1 November the NUM imposed a national overtime ban against the board's plans to close uneconomic pits. Miners were also unhappy about a 5.2 per cent pay offer. The following February rumours were rife of pit closures in Scotland and a strike was agreed at Polmaise colliery. On 1 March the miners' fears became real when the closure of Cortonwood in Yorkshire was announced, and 55,000 Yorkshire miners came out on strike.

On 6 March 'the NCB told the NUM it planned reducing output by 4,000,000 tonnes and shedding 20,000 jobs within the year, an announcement which the miners saw as a breach of the normal consultations and agreements in the industry. By 12 March the strike was made official with almost solid support from Yorkshire, Scotland and Kent. South Wales miners, at general meetings, voted by eighteen collieries to ten not to support strike action, for Arthur Scargill's motives were not fully trusted. The strike only became solid when its supporters picketed the eighteen pits which wanted to continue working. Production was halted at Merthyr Vale, where not one piece of coal was to be mined during the year long strike.

A community built around coal suddenly found its lifeline had been taken away. The area had undergone a terrible time in the 1926 strike and had suffered problems in subsequent smaller disputes and strikes in the 1970's, but this strike was to last for a year and families were about to experience, perhaps not the grinding poverty of sixty years earlier, but hardships they had never expected.

Not just mining families suffered, for the villages around the pit were heavily dependent on the colliery. 644 men were employed there, but including their families it meant 1,700 people were directly dependent on the mine for their existence, out of a total population of 4,074. Hundreds more were indirectly dependent in subsidiary businesses. With no substantial industry for miles around—the nearest employers were in Merthyr, Pontypridd and Cardiff—there was hardly a family in Merthyr Vale and Aberfan not affected in some way by the strike.

Maureen Hughes and Eunice Tovey

Eunice Tovey is now 56. Her husband Ray went underground at the age of 15 in 1947, first at Treharris, joining Merthyr Vale 14 years later. After a break from mining for twelve months during the strike, rapidly deteriorating emphysema forced him to retire shortly after the return to work.

Maureen's father followed her grandfathers and one great-grandfather into the pit at Merthyr Vale where he worked as an electrician on the surface. He left in the 1930's and moved to Essex, later returning to work in the new Hoover washing machine factory where he became a shop steward.

'He was always fighting causes and taking on people's cases if they'd been injured in work. Brought up in this background I naturally became a socialist. I didn't like the poverty and unemployment we could see around us as children. When the strike happened I saw my main contribution as being able to give support to the NUM.

'Some women would have been overwhelmed and intimidated by the union system because it was male dominated. I was used to talking to men on an equal footing as in the early 70's, when living in Essex, I became the only female labour councillor on the local council. Sometimes you found the NUM and the women's support groups didn't get on and there was no real liasion between them, but we had none of that feeling in Merthyr Vale. We were one.'

Many of the miners' wives had never involved themselves to any great extent in political issues, although most, like their husbands, came from staunch mining backgrounds and held strong social beliefs. The 1984/85 strike made many women more politically aware, at least for a while, as they fought to feed and clothe their families.

As a result more than a hundred women's support groups were formed in Wales with over 1,000 active members. Meetings were held throughout the valleys at which attendance sometimes topped 300. At Merthyr Vale a small but determined body of about 20 women created a support group to help the miners.

'The first thing the group did was to go to a demonstration at the local social security office to protest over payments. Then we raised money for the single miners who weren't able to claim any state benefits. We held sales, went carol singing and some would sing in the clubs and have a collection afterwards.'

Eunice Tovey had never been to a political meeting or been involved in any way with womens' groups, but she was angered and saddened by the poverty she saw around her during the strike and decided to take action. She joined with other women to collect money for the single miners, and also started to make door to door collections for tins of food.

Once she had become embroiled in this work she started helping the South Wales Womens Support Group, travelling to surrounding valleys like the Rhymney and the Rhondda to attend meetings. 'I was doing things then that I never thought I'd do. I started to speak out and to go to marches like the Mines not Missiles march in Oxford. I began to feel better about everything and the contacts started to open my eyes to what was happening to us.

'For the first time I was meeting women with strong political views and I started to wish I was more like that. But I surprised myself because I suddenly discovered I had leadership skills and for the first time ever a lot of women started depending on me to get things going and to organise them. People would actually wait for me to take the lead, whereas I always used to wait until everyone else had spoken first.'

Eunice believes the strike changed the outlook of the miners' wives in Merthyr Vale and Aberfan. 'The strike made me feel very bitter. It aroused feelings I had not had before. I had always been brought up in a strong Labour family and had been interested in watching political debates and things like that on television. My grandmother used to drum it into us that we should never trust the Conservatives, and told us we must always be Labour. When there were strikes before we were just at home with the kids and struggling but this time it was different, mainly because it went on for so long. We just felt we had to do something—we felt so helpless but felt we could just not stand by and do nothing, and that's when we started to try to do something for our boys. And once we had started I really thought it encouraged our men to be strong. We were behind the men every step of the way and instead of being at home complaining about what we couldn't have, we supported them.'

During the strike the Toveys would not have survived without the help of well-wishers, friends, neighbours and other families. Eunice's mother not only tried to help her but had to try and support five families in total, as she had two other daughters whose husbands were miners, as well as two sons in the pit.

As the strike started to bite, families soon had to give up on the extras in life, shortly cutting back to the bare essentials. The Toveys went from an income of £100 every week, plus their son's income, to £25 a week to keep the three of them. After three months the television on hire from a local firm had to go back as they could no longer afford the couple of pounds rent each week. Her husband put a huge card on the wall behind the empty space which read 'Watch this Space', and that's exactly all they had to watch for the next nine months.

For years the family had taken a holiday in Porthcawl and had recently started to go abroad. All holidays were cancelled. New clothes were off the shopping list for a year. Although they did not have a huge mortgage, they were unable to meet the installments and had had to go to the bank to ask them to agree to the suspension of all payments. They also had to appeal to the council to delay payments of rates.

The available money had to be concentrated on food. Every second week they would receive a small food parcel from the NUM containing a few tins of baked beans, a Fray Bentos meat pie, a few pounds of potatoes and a tin of corned beef.

'Out of that we'd make a lot of corned beef and potato pies and we'd get some faggots. Every other week when the food parcel came, it was like Christmas. What I found worst of all was a trip to the Asda superstore, where I would only put a few bare essentials in the bottom of the trolley other people would walk around with enough to feed us for a whole month. It was really terrible.'

Despite the hardships and the loss of so much including their entire social life, she never once thought of giving up. The fact that so many in the village were going through exactly the same struggle helped. 'I did not want my husband to go back to work on his own. I wanted him to be going back with all the rest, having won. As the strike continued everybody was getting so fed up and depressed that I began to fear that the men would just dwindle back and that was the last thing we wanted—everybody had to go back as one big body. But towards the end we were all near breaking point. I wanted us to stay out because there were still men in jail, but I thought the men may start to dribble back.'

During the strike her husband found a new pride in his wife. 'At least we could hold our heads up high. For the first time instead of being behind us they were right up alongside us. I liked it when she was like that, for it helped us to be strong and to carry on because if we'd have had our women nagging us back in the house it would have made it much more difficult to stay out for so long. It gave us the confidence to go on. I was proud of her and proud of what we were doing and what we were fighting for, and we were all in the same boat.'

During the strike Ray used to go on picket duty at Didcot from Monday till Wednesday. The picket money bought him a few pints and allowed him to bring home a few pounds every week. While he was away Eunice could also cut down on the amount of food she needed.

On Eunice's birthday during the strike a card he sent her said perhaps what many were forced to say. It was addressed to 'A striker's wife ... no flowers ... but lots of love.'

Maureen was keen to help on the picket line itself. 'Personally I wanted to be there to see what was happening. I wanted to support not only the miners but the village. I didn't want the community to suffer. A long time after the strike a man came up to me and said "You were the woman on the picket line—you'll never know how much that boosted morale just seeing you there supporting us." Very often I would be the only woman there.

Esme Kitto from Aberfan, who was fifty at the time of the strike and another member of the support group, remembers the unhappiness felt by some miners at the women's involvement.

'They'd always had their mothers and wives at home. They must have been worried to see their women getting shoved and pushed and abused on the picket line. I think they thought we were challenging their authority in some way and they wanted us in the shadows, supporting them but not seen.

'However it was frightening. We were usually cold and wet and we weren't having proper food, just things we could manage to buy. You became wedged in amongst the mass of people and when the line surged forward around the bend you'd get crushed against the walls of the houses at Nixonville. If somebody had fallen there would have been a tragedy as there was nothing you could have done.

'On one occasion my own son was arrested and I couldn't find out where he was for twenty-four hours. It was all very brutal. I had always respected the police before the strike and had brought up my children to also respect them and to turn to them for help. But after the strike and even now I can never look a policeman in the face. I just remember one shouting "What are you having for dinner this weekend—I'm having roast beef, all the veg and roast potatoes. You lot will be having boiled potatoes."

'I don't think the women on the picket line were treated very differently because they were women, and in some ways we took advantage of ourselves for we could give more aggro as although the police would push and shove you, they wouldn't grab you.'

Eunice's husband Ray believes the strike days, despite the hardship, were the best he can remember but he says there is no doubt that the men lost the battle and he believes the pit changed from the day they walked out. 'When the men went back, all the life had gone out of Merthyr Vale. We had lost. We had lost everything except our dignity, but I don't regret it. It showed people what trade unions were and what they meant. But afterwards there was a different feeling in the pit, for all British Coal was doing then was closing down pits to bring in cheap coal from abroad, and it caused a lot of bitterness. The strike ended the pit's future. I think it could have recovered, but the way British Coal was going about matters made it difficult. From 1984 there were closures everywhere and people were being trans-ferred to Merthyr Vale from Penallta and Penrhiwceiber and elsewhere, which broke up the comradeship that we'd had underground. The last shift I worked I was with fourteen or sixteen men—I don't think I knew half of them.'

Another thing died with the end of the strike and the end of the pit, the Womens Support Group. Eunice recalls 'I blossomed during the strike and it didn't end straight away afterwards, but I had a lot of domestic commitments, family illnesses and that sort of thing and they seemed more important. I carried on going to meet-ings for about twelve months afterwards, for the group still organised showings of videos on social issues and political topics. But fewer and fewer of us turned up till there were only about two at any meeting. The miners strike had been the issue, and now we felt we had no cause. With Ray back at work life returned to what it was before and I started to enjoy life back at home.

'Before the strike I had always been very nervous, but the strike and the role I started to play took me out of my shell. Strangely since its over, I think I've gone back into my shell once more.' Maureen, on the other hand, remains active, and served Aberfan as a Labour councillor until May 1991.

Above Pontlottyn, 1984

66

Top left: Miners on safety work, Merthyr Vale, 1984   Top right: Picketing at Llanwern, 1984
Bottom left: Dai Pigeon the day of return to work, Merthyr Vale Bottom right: Isolated scab, same day.

Opposite Merthyr Vale colliery, 1984

Gerald and Sylvia Williams

Gerald was born and raised in Merthyr Vale and joined the pit after three and a half years in the navy. He worked in the washery at the colliery from 1979 and was sent to picket Didcot power station during the strike.

Initially the miners from Merthyr Vale had been bussed for overnight stays in the Cannock Chase coalfields, the Coventry and Warwickshire pits and local coal distribution centres. But on 27 March the men were given the specific task of setting up and maintaining a picket line at Didcot. Here they worked closely with miners from Mardy whose task was to establish a support group and organise collections.

Like most miners Gerald was at first apprehensive about picketing in a conservative area where he believed people would not want to help or listen to them. But his time in Oxford was to change his life in a completely unexpected way, for he met his wife to be.

'The first night there was no shelter at all and we all had to sleep on the bus. Then we noticed a man who came past every day with wooden pallets and we made two shacks out of these and plastic sheeting to keep out the heavy rain and wind, because that winter we saw some of the coldest weather for thirty years, with temperatures at one point reaching minus fourteen degrees celsius. But it didn't deter us.' Accommodation was soon provided by supporters in Ruskin College.

'At first the National Union of railwaymen supported us and it was fine to watch the mountain of coal inside go down. But then the coal lorries started coming. Most of the drivers were from Wales and perhaps there would be just four or eight of us outside. There was nothing we could do to stop them, they just rumbled past.

'One day in June, after I had been picketing as usual, I went to a dance in the Headington Labour Club where I met Sylvia, who was working part-time in a shoe shop. Within weeks I proposed to her and spent all my spare time away from the picket line with her. Sometimes she would even join me on the picket.'

In December they married at a time when the effects of the strike were really beginning to hurt the miners. 'A lot of people in both families thought we should wait but it was an incredible day. We obviously didn't have a great deal of money and I didn't want it to be a huge affair, but his mates and the people he'd made friendships with in Oxford helped make the day wonderful' recalls Sylvia.

'The picket duty bus was laid on to bring Gerald's family from Merthyr Vale, the cake was made by the cooks from Ruskin College who had befriended Gerald and the miners from Wales. And the boys who had been picketing all came along. In the end there were two hundred of us there on the night.'

Meanwhile the miners made contacts with groups potentially sympathetic to their aims. They organised a mass meeting at the Austin Rover factory, met with doctors, ambulance drivers, teachers, print workers and many other unions in the area. At a meeting with the Fire Brigades Union a bell sounded calling the firemen out to an emergency. They went out, dealt with the fire, and returned to find the miners still on their feet speaking.

Mike Richards from Mardy colliery recalls the other side of the work, collecting food and money and helping gather support. 'The men helped with collecting food parcels and were surprised at some of the items handed in on their door to door rounds, including a tin of Hungarian croquettes with the cooking instructions written in French, and a carton of Biactol spot cleaning lotion. A bottle of wine and six glasses were handed in with the words "to be drunk by a miner" written on a note.

Mike Richards

'One day the wife of a policeman who was on picket duty in Nottingham came and gave us a huge box of food. She didn't agree with the strike but said she had seen the terrible violence on the television and was upset. She obviously knew other policemen and what had been happening. We would have calls from people saying to come to their homes to pick up food and they'd leave it outside their doors. We never saw their faces. One day we were called to a house with an orchard owned by a Polish couple. She had picked hundreds of apples for us and every one had been wrapped in a little piece of paper.'

Street collections became both a major source of income, with up to a quarter of passers-by making donations, and a way of putting across the miners' cause. Although generally peaceful and involving 25 to 30 people each week, Ted Syd, a retired man who collected at Tescos, was kicked and injured quite badly. Also at Tescos, on two occasions, young people were attacked and bruised by hostile right-wingers.

Mike Richards recalls 'that you couldn't just go out on the streets with your tins and collect money—you'd be arrested by the police. You were only allowed to collect for a cause on one specified day of the year in the city centre, and once a week in outlying areas. As the council was controlled by Labour they arranged permits for us to collect in different areas. The Tories did what they could to oppose these moves and towards the end of the strike one Tory councillor complained to the police about the legality of food collections.' Miners jokingly tell how they were warned that it was an arrestable offence to knock on people's doors, but after gaining legal advice, carried on without further problems.

The miners also determined to gain the backing of the students, but in many cases faced extremely hostile receptions. At Queen's College Mike Richards was advised not to eat in the hall with the students before addressing a meeting of the Junior Common Room, because of fears he would be pelted with food.

A motion from the floor that night proposed 'A nail be driven through Arthur Scargill's toupee and that a sack of the president's urine be sent to him to drink.' Mike Richards walked out in protest. The motion was defeated and £500 was eventually raised by the college.

Another recommendation from some students was that 'This JCR thoroughly recommends the striking miners put down their pint glasses, get off their backsides and get back to work where they can earn their exorbitant wages and start to pay back money given to them during the strike,' continuing

'This JCR

1) Regards the striking miners as overpaid lazy slobs.

2) Urges the government to withdraw all welfare benefits (including mortgage payments) from striking miners.'

However, confronted by the evidence and gaining knowledge of the mining communities, every college in Oxford ended up giving some money to the miners.

There were two Christmas parties held in Aberfan thanks to the people of Oxford. Food was transported from the city and all children were given a present. The first party was held the day after the taxi driver was killed bringing workers into Merthyr Vale. It was immediately feared by villagers that the people from Oxford would change their minds and not come, but the party was a bright event in what was otherwise a tragic weekend. The Oxford Community Arts Group and the women from Greenham Common provided the entertainment. Hundreds of presents were wrapped and when the women found stickers on the boys' tool sets which read 'Just Like Dad's', they swapped them for NUM stickers.

Before the second party the miners took a vanful of Oxford supporters to the top of the mountain above Aberfan where they stood looking down on the graves of all the children who had died in the disaster.

Apart from this moral and personal support, during the strike the people of Oxford raised more than £100,000 to help the Welsh valley miners.

Picketing at Didcot

At the end of the strike Gerald and Sylvia settled in Merthyr Vale and Gerald became a member of the NUM lodge committee. But by 1988 he realised that the village no longer held a future for him. 'The pit had changed. It had once been a very happy place but after the strike it was completely different. To move was a terrible decision to make, but I had to think about my future, so we sold up and went back to Oxford where I took a job with the post office. We created a whole new life, we had to. As it turned out we made the right choice. We were able to sell our house, but if you think of 600 people trying to sell their house at the same time when a pit finally closes, it's a lot harder. We sold ours to an English couple as did our neighbours opposite, and that further changes the community.'

But Gerald is anxious to return to Wales. 'The thing I miss most is the friendship. Here after all these years we still call our neighbours Mr and Mrs. At home you could just go through the door at any time and have a cup of tea and a chat.'

Sylvia too misses Wales. 'I see Merthyr Vale as my home and I break my heart when after a visit we have to come back to Oxford. When I first knew Gerald I knew nothing about Welsh people or miners. Gerald was rough and ready—he had hair down to the middle of his back. At first he just seemed jokey and friendly but as I got to know him I realised how serious and dedicated he was about the strike. I didn't perhaps understand it all at first. In Oxford you might not always get the job you want, but there's always a job. I couldn't imagine how one industry could be so important to so many people.'

Sylvia is determined to set up their own home in Wales but knows Merthyr Vale can offer little in the way of employment. Within the next 5 years they are planning to make a home in Swansea where they can afford to buy their own house.

Picketing at Didcot

Merthyr Vale, 1984

73

Aberfan, 1984

74

Glyn Rogers

Chief Superintendent Glyn Rogers was the police divisional commander for Merthyr and the Rhymney valley from January 1982. He was in charge of policing the Merthyr Vale picket lines during much of the strike, retiring in February 1985 just before the strike ended. He was instructed by the Chief Constable of South Wales to ensure that miners wishing to work were able to enter and leave the pit in safety.

'Politics didn't enter into it as far as I was concerned. We had two men wanting to work and it was my duty to ensure that anyone who wanted to work was allowed to.'

That was how he saw his role in the strike, but a deep division was created between police and miners as the dispute dragged on. The bitterness of men who had been without money and decent food for so many months was inevitably turned against the police who were seen as a heavy force being used and manipulated by the government to try and break the strike.

During the strike Glyn Rogers started work at 2.30 every morning to ensure his men were in place. His duties meant he was working until 6 every evening and it's ironic how much his life became like that of a miner. 'I virtually never saw the light of day. I went into work in the dark and came home in the dark.

'The sound of the picket line is something that will always stay with me. It was like a scene from the film Zulu ... zoom, zoom, zoom as the Zulus were hitting their shields. There always seemed to be an incessant noise from the miners, like the hubbub perhaps you'd get at Cardiff Arms Park for a rugby international.

'When the taxi which used to bring men to work arrived there was a surge from the miners as we tried to do our job and they did theirs. I wouldn't suggest that there weren't at times a few fists flying and sometimes there were small incidents of physical violence, that was the nature of the beast. But in my opinion there was never any real violence or antagonism. I felt I had built up a good rapport with the lodge secretary Bill King and I hope we had respect for each other and for what we both had to do.

'At the beginning it seemed as if everybody was on their best behaviour but then an air of frustration seemed to creep over the miners—perhaps they could see what they were standing for wasn't working out. They were getting stroppy and as the strike continued for month after month, they became more abusive.

'I tried to be impartial with the striking miners and with those who wanted to work—that was my job. But I thought it was awful to see men having to go to such an extent to prove a point. They were making a lot of sacrifices and I thought it was unfortunate that we were seen as an instrument to prevent them from obtaining their goal.'

The large number of police officers used on picket lines became bitterly resented by miners and communities alike who felt themselves swamped by such a force.

'You might think it was wrong to use 250 policemen, but that's democracy, if it needed 250 for those men to go in that's what was done. If they'd been stopped from going in mob rule would have won the day.' Glyn Rogers admits this caused some animosity towards his men, but he feels his officers would have been happier without the strike and the extra pay it brought.

'It is likely that some miners felt provoked by the police. I couldn't keep my eye on 200 or so policemen on a wet and miserable morning at 3 a.m. but by and large I think it was quite peaceful although the miners thought we were on the side of the NCB. But remember a lot of the officers knew miners on the picket line personally, even though we had officers brought in from as far away as Bridgend and Pontypridd. You'd have people who had gone to school together, whilst some of the police officers came from mining families. I don't think there was any bitterness within the police, indeed it was painful for my officers who had never experienced anything like it—they'd never felt the abuse and bitterness on such a scale. I think a number were overawed for it's not an easy thing to see 400 pickets shouting, swearing at and reviling you. I was proud of the restraint shown by my men, often under tremendous provocation.'

When the taxi driver carrying miners to work was killed as a result of a concrete block dropped from a bridge onto his car, the atmosphere changed. 'It was no longer just the shove of the picket line and the odd fist being thrown here and there. This was a new dimension—someone had been killed and we all had to think about the effect that was going to have on the future. I was apalled that someone's life had to be forfeit to prove a point, right or wrong. But the miners felt, perhaps, that they'd lost a battle but a war had still to be won.

'It seems such a waste looking back on that period. I'm not speaking politically, I'm not a political animal. People must be allowed to strike but I felt there must be a more civilised way to deal with something that led to such misery and even death.

'I don't think anyone could have anything but the deepest respect for the tenacity the miners showed. One had to have real courage to go on strike depriving one's family of so much for so long.'

Ivor & Jamie, Merthyr Vale colliery, 1985

Merthyr Vale

Peter Davies

Peter decided not to work underground having been made aware of the difficulties and dangers of mining and being brought up near the coughing and wheezing of miners suffering from silicosis. Though most of his male relatives had been miners, he was fortunate to have studied at university and become a teacher. His feelings about the colliery were a mixture of concern at the deaths and disease caused by the work, and a belief that the jobs, wages, and the community spirit engendered by a mine, were worth keeping.

He was a councillor on Merthyr Borough Council between 1979 and 1987 where, during the strike, he exerted his influence on behalf of the miners, also joining the picket line. He later wrote about his experiences in a book which he dedicated to the miners of Merthyr Vale.

'The first phase of the strike lasted from early March until the third week in November and was quiet and for the main part uneventful. Meetings were held and collections taken. The only activity appeared to be down at the land sales yard and Jacky McGinty's patch where concessionary coal was being handled. The hot summer and peaceful times at the pit made the strike seem a million miles away; Orgreave where there were confrontations between police and pickets appeared unreal.'

But the effects of the strike soon started to trickle home. 'News reached us of the arrests of Merthyr Vale miners in various places, including England, names of boys we knew. Savings started to run out and there would be no holidays this year. The food parcels being distributed seemed pitiful in relation to a family's needs, but the men carried on with the task of giving a little to those who needed so much. But in London Mrs. Thatcher and the Tory government preached about the evils of the miners and the need to make them feel the effects of what they were doing.'

The 1980 Employment Act allowed the government to assume miners were receiving £15 a week strike pay and to deduct the equivalent amount from any social security benefits. 'Whole families were made to live on £12 or less a week. The collections made around Merthyr Vale ward could do very little to help most families, but they did provide money without which the situation would have been much worse. The collections also allowed something else to happen, it allowed people to identify with the miners. During the whole time we collected from house to house only six people refused to donate. More important were the comments from people of all ages, but especially the elderly. I'll never forget the proud, elderly men and women who often thrust £5 notes into our tins and when we protested they'd simply say "Their fight is our fight." It made us feel very humble but it also gave us and the miners strength to face the criticisms being levelled against the strikers by the media and people not part of a mining community.'

As winter neared the community was to face new hardships, though with some extra help. 'Although the sun was still shining it was getting on to autumn and there was a nip in the air. Men's trainers were wearing out; whilst unbelievably there was not enough coal to burn and concessionary coal claimants began to experience diffi-culties. It seemed that matters were going to worsen as winter approached.

'Mid Glamorgan County Council gave free meals to the children and Merthyr Borough Council gave some money to the relief fund, but many felt it was too bloody little, and too bloody late.

'Then suddenly two men wished to go into the colliery. The first day of the scabs going in was one of shock mingled with incredulity that anyone could think more of money than their fellow workers and community. I can remember them hidden in their anoraks or under a coat lying down in the transit van.

'The first day they returned, 14 December, they failed to gain entry when 300 pickets arrived. But the next day the police arrived in force and they were able to enter the pit. From then on the tension mounted as the police tried to prevent pick-eting miners from coming anywhere near the pit.

'I remember the dark glow of Nixonville with the oily yellow lamps casting gloomy shadows, and pickets huddled in donkey jackets, duffels, anoraks and the inevitable cap, hat or bobble. Our yellow stick-on badges were everywhere. We were lined up near the houses, by the fitter's shed or alongside the office block, but not across the entrance; that was police territory. That and the road, with row upon row of black coated, black hatted figures goading the strikers by saying "a few more pounds for the holidays", whilst others held up £10 notes from the protection of their vans.

'I also remember vividly the practiced shove of the pickets, reminiscent of a rugby match, and the realisation, as a cold shock, that the shove and push were designed to reach the van and its occupants. The pickets nearly did reach it twice.

'Then there was the violence of the mass picket and the frightening speed of action and the rapidity with which events unfolded in the space of a few minutes. The men from Maerdy were real professionals the way they rolled the police around and against the wall. There were scenes of uncontrolled violence as stones flew over the canteen, concrete block fencing was torn down and there was the horror of seeing and hearing baying police dogs within the yard.

'We were shocked to see road blocks being formed at the bottom of Bridge Street and on Bell's Hill. Similar ones were set up at Pentrebach and Edwardsville, all to prevent men being able to picket at their own colliery. The road blocks were extended and the number of pickets dwindled as men faced a seven or eight mile walk at 5 o'clock in the morning, all on a striker's diet.'

To the miners and villagers the police presence in Aberfan seemed overwhelming, even angering and confusing people not directly involved. A packed public meeting decided to organise a community petition asking for police activity to be reduced. This took place on the eve of a meeting the chief constable was due to have with the local council to discuss the same problem. But suddenly these meetings and petitions paled into insignificance for word came through of a tragedy that was to shake the mining fraternity throughout the country. The anger had spilled over and David Wilkie, a taxi driver bringing a miner to the colliery, had been killed when a concrete block was dropped from a bridge through the windscreen of his car.

There was a huge debate in the community over whether the miners responsible should have been charged with murder. Many felt it was an innocent prank aimed at simply stopping the taxi but which had gone badly wrong. Some felt the charge was brought for political considerations to divert public sympathy.

Whatever, it did mark or coincide with the turning point in the wider strike, as public support edged away. Picketing continued throughout the harsh winter relatively uneventfully, except for times when a big push would be announced and pickets would arrive out of the darkness from everywhere to show that the solidarity and strength was still there.

Then at the beginning of February began the third and final phase. Though the strike was holding pretty solid in South Wales, miners were starting to drift back elsewhere in the country. Locally, thoughts began to turn to the future of South Wales in general and of Merthyr Vale in particular. Relations with the police deteriorated, the police even ceasing to try to talk to the miners. Peter Davies says 'This whole short period was rather like someone standing watching the tide go out, and not knowing what would happen next—would it come back?'

But it did, in a return to work. 'Men suddenly appeared in their orange overalls, white hats and big boots, and the wheels began turning. The pit and community was alive again, but with words to remind us of the dangers the men faced. The words Tom O'Brien, a retired miner and now a county councillor, said to his brother Frank. "Take care boy, you'll have to get used to her again. Go easy now."'

The wrecked taxi near Rhymney Bridge, 30 November 1984

The return to work, with Bill King in his cap under the banner

Bill King

Bill had dreamt of becoming a radio officer in the merchant navy, but to achieve that he needed to gain an education, which he started by winning a scholarship to the local grammar school. His father was laid off from his job as a steelworker at Dowlais in 1927 and didn't find another job till 1940. Bill was the oldest boy still at home out of seven children and by 1935 was acutely aware of the financial struggle his family was facing to keep him in school. He successfully applied to the mayor of Merthyr for a pair of boots from a special fund, but his deputy headmaster denied they ever arrived.

Angry and embarrassed he decided to leave and went underground at Glyn-Neath colliery, giving most of his pay to his parents. When the colliery closed in 1940 he worked in the valleys building and camouflaging factories before joining the Royal Navy. After the war he returned to mining at Aberpergwm colliery in West Glamorgan and became more and more involved in the NUM. He finally became full time NUM lodge secretary at Merthyr Vale, where he stayed until his retirement on his 65th birthday just after the end of the miners strike.

Bill King well remembers the day the taxi driver was killed. 'The night before the men from Mountain Ash had walked over the mountain by candlelight to bring support to the men of Merthyr Vale. I met them at the pit in the morning, but there was some kind of pall over the whole area. There was something in the air. Then Superintendent Rogers came up to me and said there's no need to continue, there's no-one coming in today. I knew straight away what he was going to tell me. Ivor and Dai reached over and said something's happened, something serious has happened in Rhymney.

'The superintendent confirmed this but wouldn't say what and asked me to go to the police station. Even then I feared I might be snatched and warned the boys to find a solicitor if I wasn't back soon. I went up to the station in a Jag and as soon as I reached it the head of CID said "Look now, a man has been killed. You are the leader of the gang so you know all about it" and demanded to know what had happened. He released me still saying he wanted to know in twenty-four hours who had done it and who had planned it.'

Bill didn't know the answer; the police launched a massive investigation and soon tracked down the miners responsible in the nearby community of Rhymney. The event changed everything at Merthyr Vale. The tide of sympathy in many parts of the country turned against the miners, people even accusing them of murder.

The taxi driver's family found their life turned upside down by a dispute which had nothing to do with them, whilst two young men with no political inclinations were caught up in the fever of a strike that was becoming more and more difficult to endure, and spent the next four years in prison.

Bill King recalls the initial court case. 'As sentence was passed the two boys shuddered, they just came together rocking. Girls who were in court were screaming and fainting, when the judge simply said "Clear the court" and they were dragged outside. The original murder charge was reduced to manslaughter on appeal and when we returned to work we organised a pithead collection each week. Many people would put in a pound or two from their wages and we were collecting around £140 a week for a trust fund created at the Pontypridd headquarters for the boys to have when they came out.'

Another day of mixed emotions for Bill was the first day back at work after the strike was over. 'We had said we would never go back beaten and that our return would be victorious with drums beating and bands playing. In fact our return was a cold and quiet one for we decided not to have bands or music as we didn't want to wake up the community that had given us so much backing all the time we were out. They'd put up with enough noise and disturbance so kindly during the strike.

'I was really miserable but had to keep a brave face to lead the men back in. It was a long three-quarters of a mile walk back into that pit. I felt we had lost the strike, for we hadn't gained anything except the amazing experience and the wonderful involvement we had had with the community. At least it did serve to educate people who hadn't understood anything about the fight before. People's lives were changed irreversibly by that strike.

'But despite the way I felt everybody was excited and it was as if they were high on drugs going back in that day. They felt they'd lost but wanted to go back in, so we had to go back saying it was a victory for ordinary people. We were going back into the real world.

'It was dark and very cold and everything was quiet. With us were people from all over the country and as we walked there were about three hundred of us. Students had come from Ruskin College and supporters had travelled from Didcot to walk with us, and a lot of the local people who had been so good got up to walk with us. But I knew we'd lost the fight, and my carrier bag was empty.'

During the strike Bill had never been seen without a plastic carrier bag which he carried with him wherever he went. People believed it carried the Coal not Dole stickers that were sported on practically every coat and jacket in South Wales. In fact soon after the strike began and the threat to the union's funds became real, Bill was ordered to remove all cash from the Merthyr Vale lodge bank account. He took out the £28,000 and from then on he kept it in the fragile carrier bag he carried around.

'We had had a few break-ins at houses near where I lived so I was frightened of leaving it at home. At one time a friend of mine who managed a bank allowed me to keep it in a case lodged in a safety box. There was no fear of sequestration as no outsiders knew he had the money in his bag and he was confident it would be safe with the local bank. But it soon became obvious as I went in nearly every day to take out some money for a hardship case or to pay another bill that the bank didn't like it. So it went back into the carrier bag and there it stayed.'

The dwindling supply of money was taken on picket duty to Merthyr Vale every morning, to Didcot when Bill was on duty away and to every meeting he had with the police and the local council. The money comprised the 5 per cent of members' union payments returned to each lodge. It had to help with hardship cases, children's parties and the high administration costs the NUM faced during a year long strike, including the cost of transport to picket lines in England. It was also used to buy provisions for food parcels.

'At night I used to hide it under my pillow but you can imagine what it was like sleeping on all those fifty and twenty pound notes, including fifty pounds worth of fifty pence pieces. During the day a few of the lads who knew what was in the bag always kept close. I was never on my own and was always with a car load of people. If we had to go to a meeting in Cardiff on union business the lads always stuck near me—they knew I would have enough money to buy us a cup of tea!

'The day we went back there wasn't a single penny in the carrier bag. There was no money to pay for administration and nothing to help pay for any retirement parties that were coming up. It was traditional to buy a miner's lamp and have a little get together for whoever was going, but there was no money left.

'That morning as we were about to walk in, Maureen Hughes of the Women's Support Group came up to me and gave me £500 in cash to start the fund up again. They'll never know how much that was appreciated.'

The Merthyr Vale lodge had instructed Bill to vote against a return at the South Wales conference called to discuss the strike. The lodge was concerned about the men who'd been arrested, imprisoned and sacked for there was no agreement about their futures. But there was also growing concern in South Wales that unless there was an organised return to work, the strike would start to crumble and people would have drifted back anyway. Secret meetings were already being held not far from the pit to discuss an unofficial return to work.

'The men had been living from hand to mouth from the August before. With hindsight I think that we could have gone back then, for we didn't achieve any more by staying out longer. But the strike had turned into a political crusade. When we came out on strike I think there was a general feeling in the country that we were moving on to better things. By the end of the strike we realised that that wasn't true and the feeling had gone.

'It was perhaps the hardest time, going back. While we were all out we had all been in the same boat; none of us had any money but nobody was talking about their financial problems. I knew when we went back it would be harder than anything.

'Most miners are always one pay away from bankruptcy. Money goes as quickly as it's earned and if a miner has a good week pay-wise, he has a good week spending. While we were on strike we couldn't afford to pay for holidays, Christmas clubs, clothes and things like that, but when we went back it changed and the pressures returned. Building societies and banks wanted their money, as there was rent and mortgages to be paid, not only then but to cover the last year as well. As soon as we got our first pay packet everybody wanted a bit of it. It was a depressing time.'

Closure

In November 1988 British Coal's group general manager Terence Wheatley warned that Merthyr Vale was making too great a loss. He urged that output must be improved as it was 2,500 tonnes a week below the 7,500 target required to break even, and he told the unions that despite an investment of £13 million in recent years 'the results are proving to be very disappointing and Merthyr Vale is making losses on a scale which cannot be tolerated at a time when the mining industry is exposed to the most severe financial pressure brought about by competition from low cost world traded coal.'

He warned that unless output from the new super face was improved he would have to take a second look at the project. By March 1989 output had increased allowing Merthyr Vale to be withdrawn from the review list, but the miners were told that it now had to produce 8,100 tonnes a week as losses in the current financial year had already reached £6.63 million. The miners accepted the challenge, but were hampered by geological problems and production was only increased from 5,271 to just 5,800 tonnes a week. As a result in April they were given only three weeks to break even or face closure.

On 18 May British Coal stated the mine would face another review on 9 June, as a result of which on 17 July it announced plans to close Merthyr Vale since the production target of 8,100 tonnes had still not been reached. That same week the local Hoover factory announced around 100 redundancies.

Three days after the announcement of the pit's closure, the men held a mass meeting and more than 400 miners present decided to fight the closure, with only 10 men voting to accept it. British Coal's existing redundancy scheme, due to end on 26 August, gave a man with twenty years service £30,000 if he accepted immediate redundancy, but only £5,000 after 26 August if they chose to fight and lost, or such terms as were to be set out in a new redundancy arrangement then being discussed in parliament. British Coal defended itself against charges of blackmail by saying that they had announced the end of the scheme way back the previous November. The miners, unsurprisingly, felt the closure announcement and the end of the redundancy arrangements were carefully co-ordinated to put maximum pressure on the miners to accept British Coal's plans without a fight.

On Wednesday 23 August British Coal announced the pit would close that weekend and Friday 25 August 1989 became the last day that coal was mined at Merthyr Vale.

Treharris, 1990

The traditional Miners' Holiday destination, Porthcawl, 1990

Merthyr Vale, 1990

Tony Davies and Peter Evans

Peter Evans had, at the age of 9, watched his father die from pneumonoconiosis and had vowed never to go underground. However the lure of the pit and the money offered proved too great and he was fortunate to win an electrical apprenticeship at Deep Dyffryn in the Cynon valley. When it closed in 1979 he was transferred with 138 men to Merthyr Vale, where, having been chairman of the NUM lodge at Deep Dyffryn, he was put on that at Merthyr Vale to try to help integrate the men. He is still working in the mines, coordinating electricity supplies to the remaining pits.

Tony Davies was the NUM Lodge Secretary at Merthyr Vale, where he had been moved following the closure of Blaensychan in Pontypool, from 1985 until closure. When he joined the pit there were more than 800 men working at Merthyr Vale, many working on seam B32. This was proving to be an excellent source of steam coal being sold all over Britain for solid fuel domestic central heating systems, and for industrial use. Then in 1986 a serious explosion at the pit put the face out of action.

'Fortunately nobody was killed but the blast blew men off their feet a mile away from the seam. If the fire had ignited the coal-dust the whole pit would have been closed, but even as it was the face was flooded and closed for good, leaving us just two faces.'

Peter Evans feels that British Coal's enquiry never did reveal the real reason behind the explosion, fearing it would be made public. 'We had two sets of fans but one would be knocked off when people weren't working there in order to save money. At first there was no problem with the system and every Sunday night before the shift came back on duty after the weekend firemen would enter the district to test for any build up of methane gas. If over 1.25 per cent was found in the air the chambers would be opened up to flush out the gas. But just before the explosion there was a major electrical storm during which we lost our main power supply to the colliery which meant that the main fan went off, effectively leaving both fan systems out of business.

'What caused the spark to ignite the build up of gas isn't clear. It was likely to be either an underground fall of stone or perhaps a faulty switch created a spark when the power was restored. Either way the result was the explosion. British Coal made the decision to flood the district, so we were never really able to find out exactly what happened.'

After the explosion the men carried on working the B51 and V40 districts but they were getting so much coal from the area that according to Tony Davies the pit could not cope with the amount. To solve the problem the NUM asked for a proper winding system to be installed, but at first the application was rejected.

The new skip winding gear was eventually installed in 1987 and new production targets were set which the men struggled to reach. However they were never able to produce as much coal following the explosion and a number of reorganisations took place, gradually reducing the pit's manpower until only 540 men were left.

According to Tony Davies the first hint of closure came in 1987. 'We were called to a review meeting and were told we had made money that month. The area director told us to carry on the way we were, saying we were not going to make a fortune at the pit, but we were doing alright, and that new investment would be forthcoming which would produce returns quite quickly.'

In 1988 despite the serious problems developing at the pit British Coal continued putting money in, investing £4.3 million in a new coal washery.

'Everything was pretty quiet until the next review meeting at the end of 1988. Then we were told that the only future for us was to go over to retreat mining. In effect we were told Merthyr Vale was going to be a one face pit and that retreat mining would make it profitable.' Retreat mining involves driving roadways into the area of coal to be worked and then working backwards cutting out the coal in one block as the machinery is pulled away. In this way the coal is removed quickly leaving the roof to fall as the miners retreat.

'We argued with British Coal that it was not a good idea to rely on one face and said we needed to have a spare face, for retreat mining is very expensive and you need a standby in case things go wrong. We were only 50 metres away from completing the road to the face when the closure decision came. Everyone visiting the face had said it was one of the best in the South Wales coalfield, and still this blow came. Even then retreat mining could have saved more than half the jobs.

'It was a political decision to shut the colliery, for they kept setting targets, and when we kept reaching them by working three shifts a day, they would move them up again. We were on the verge of coming into profit when they took the brutal decision to close us down. They wanted twenty-five cuts of coal from the face every week and we reached twenty-three. We were just two cuts short but even that wasn't enough for them. (A cut involves mining a section of coal about 210 metres long by 80 centimetres wide.)

'We have decided to move ahead immediately with a scheme to develop three million tonnes of coal in the eastern side of the mine which will provide security in Merthyr Vale into the twenty-first century. This is very encouraging news not only for Merthyr Vale but for the South Wales coalfield. It shows that the board is prepared to continue to give us capital for investment. It is essential to make sure that investment capital is devoted to projects which have a proven potential, as we have been able to illustrate with our recent investment schemes. Merthyr Vale, for example, has earned this additional help. Its productivity is high and relations between management and union are traditionally good.'

Phillip Weekes. South Wales Area Director, British Coal

'Merthyr Vale has lost £1.9 million already in 1989, £7.1 million last year and aggregate losses of £33.5 million since 1980. Between April and June alone the pit has lost £1 million. The pit last made a profit eight years ago despite £10 million of investment in recent years. The coalfield as a whole has lost £14 million during the April to June period.'

Terence Wheatley. South Wales Area Director, British Coal

'It was a ridiculous situation. Right up until the end we had men earning £180 a week bonus on a self-financing bonus scheme, that shows how well we were doing and how good production was. Since the end of the strike they had invested £5 million into the pit and if they had given us a chance, that would have been repaid within a year. The month before the closure the pit still made a £40,000 loss, but even the manager told us that by the next month we would be breaking even. But British Coal knew that if it could close Merthyr Vale after what they had done to Aberfan, they could close any pit anywhere in the country. They knew they would then be able to pick out the rest.

'Fifteen years of easy coal was there to be had. With the retreat face in operation we could have have produced 10,000 tonnes of saleable coal a week with profits of between £4 and £5 million a year. We volunteered a scheme which would have put 200 men out of work but would have saved the rest of the pit, and we put our figures to Terence Wheatley, the area manager. But he actually told us that even though he thought we were sincere he was not prepared to go on because he said the men were no good. I've worked in five pits and the men in Merthyr Vale were as good as any throughout the coalfield. But over the last twelve to eighteen months the heart went out of the men because they were constantly under pressure, not knowing from day to day whether they would lose their jobs. Although the majority wanted to try to save the pit, there was a small minority who did not.'

The men had been told that British Coal's redundancy scheme would end on 28 August and that there was no other scheme planned to replace it. 'It was a terrible time—I had women phoning me up at home saying I was trying to cheat their husbands and families out of up to £25,000 redundancy money. I knew there would be another scheme coming along, I was sure of it, but I could not swear on my heart that the money would be there. What could I do. It was terrible.

'During the last meeting the men decided the fight the closure and the union took the decision back to headquarters to tell British Coal that they would fight their case through the review procedure, even though no other pit in Britain, let alone South Wales, had ever been successful. But British Coal repeated that they planned to close the pit and warned that the redundancy money was coming to an end. There was so much concern amongst the men that we had to have another vote and we lost by just a few votes.

'There was an outcry because of the propaganda that British Coal had been sending out. Every single miner had a letter brought to his home telling him the

'Terence Wheatley is an outsider sent to do a hatchet job. Despite all the hard work by miners, pits are being given no chance. Every miner in South Wales, and the rest of Britain, is now living in fear of his job. We have lost 3,500 mining jobs in South Wales in less than six months. Merthyr Vale will be viable by the end of the year and the closure plan is disgusting, deplorable and an insult to the men. This is one of the worst acts of vandalism I've witnessed.'

Des Dutfield. President, South Wales NUM

redundancy scheme closed that week, and in the end the men were pressurised and frightened into believing that unless they accepted closure straight away, they would lose all the benefits for which they had worked for all those years. If they went to the review they would lose all their entitlements which frightened them to death, particularly knowing the fight they would have on their hands and the way the odds were horribly stacked against them.

'Within two days of the vote being taken and the lodge reporting back to British Coal, the pit was closed. There was no time to adjust or for a run down, no time for a bereavement or for the families to become used to it. Men who had worked underground since they were just fifteen were suddenly out of a job, with absolutely no hope of finding suitable alternative work, or even any kind of a job.'

Sadly, if the men had fought the closure plan and had lost they would still have been better off. They'd have kept their jobs for several months while the lengthy process was completed, and within months British Coal did announce a new redundancy scheme which offered terms which could have even left some men £10,000 better off.

'I didn't blame the men, but I just felt very sick. I was physically and mentally sick. I knew British Coal had won, they had frightened the men with the fear of their money. I can't even blame the men for their fears were genuine and real, but the pit and its workforce was treated with utter contempt, and there was no period to help us all adjust.

'Men went from earning £170 a week plus a bonus of £180, to jobs in factories bringing home less than £100 a week.

'Ryans, an international mining company, were interested in taking over the pit with up to 250 men, but British Coal dropped them from the contractors list. They weren't even prepared to talk to them. Looking at it as a business proposition I and some others would have been prepared to sink our redundancy money in their scheme.'

Tony says that most of the men aged over 45 have not found new jobs, though the younger ones and skilled electricians have found work elsewhere. Some of the unskilled workers have taken low paid and often seasonal jobs in factories like OP Chocolates. Others have gone into the Hoover factory to make washing machines, but by early 1991 there were problems there too. In February and March the firm announced it was having to make up to 600 redundancies, roughly a third of its workforce, due to high interest rates and the associated slump.

Top left: Deep Navigation colliery, 1990   Top right: In the safety cage, Merthyr Vale, 1986
Bottom left: Deep Navigation, 1990   Bottom right: David Holly, Deep Navigation, 1990

Completing safety work, Merthyr Vale, 1990

Taff Merthyr colliery, Treharris, 1990

Young mother, 1990

Heineken lorry, Aberfan, 1990

99

Philip Déath, Deep Navigation, 1990

Ted Rowlands

At the age of 26 Ted Rowlands became the youngest MP in the 1966 parliament when he was elected for Cardiff North. However he had a majority of just over 600 and lost the seat in the general election of June 1970. In 1971 he was chosen as the labour candidate for Merthyr, winning the nomination against Bill King. This could have caused a rift between him and the pit, but Bill King openly welcomed the new candidate.

Ted Rowlands won the seat in a by-election in 1972 and has been MP for Merthyr Tydfil ever since. He knows the area well, having been born in Porthcawl, and living in Treorchy and the Rhondda before settling in Merthyr.

'Merthyr Vale in the 1970's was very much a community pit. I can remember addressing a meeting of miners in the pit canteen during the elections of 1974 in the safe knowledge that everybody there was a constituent. By 1983 it was astonishing how the character had changed, for more than half of the men were from different valleys.'

Soon after he was elected came the strikes of 1972 and 1974. But these were minor compared to that of 1984 and its potential consequences. During this strike he helped on the picket line, and sacrificed family ties.

'The nightmarish occurrence during the strike when a man was killed was for me the turning point. The chief constable telephoned me at home at 6 a.m. to say something terrible had happened. From that time on everybody was questioning where we were going. I don't think people lost sympathy for the miners, but everybody realised we couldn't go on like this.'

It was at this point that Ted Rowlands became estranged from his cousin Phillip Weekes who was then area director of the South Wales coalfield. 'He had been an understanding manager and it aggrieved me sadly to see him being forced into obeying Macgregor's tactics. I made a public and personal appeal to him to call off the heavy policing which was being carried out just to get two people into work, for which the village was being taken over.

'After the strike pit closures started almost immediately in Wales. However for 18 months I felt the four pits in my constituency—Merthyr Vale, Deep Navigation, Trelewis Drift and Taff Merthyr—were safe. Merthyr Vale had been receiving massive investment; it even had a new transport network because people were complaining that the coal was being carried by road, damaging and dirtying their homes. We also knew there were large reserves, and closure just didn't seem feasible.

'In 1986 after the first wave of closures a deputation from the Labour party went to see Peter Walker, then Secretary of State for Energy and subsequently Secretary of State for Wales, to discuss our fears. He said that after the current restructuring of the coalfield was complete the rest of the core group of pits that remained would form a successful coalfield.

'He rubbed our noses in the high levels of capital investment going into the pits. What could we say with assurances like that. So until 1987 I was reasonably confident that I would be the M.P. representing the last core of pits in South Wales.

'But then came the sudden announcement of the closure of Lady Windsor colliery in the Cynon Valley. I think you can trace the next sad phase of closures to the arrival of Terence Wheatley as area director. I believe he was sent here as a hatchet man and it was then alarm bells started to ring. Another pit in Michael Foot's constituency closed, Marine colliery, and Tony Davies the NUM secretary at Merthyr Vale came to see me. He said he didn't like the feel of it and although at that time there was no definite threat we had this fear about Merthyr Vale and we decided to put our case early.

'We felt we needed some political cover and together with Neil Kinnock we met Terence Wheatley to talk about Merthyr Vale's future. We talked about working practices and were prepared to bend over backwards to do anything to save the pit. But from then on if targets weren't met to the minute and to the tonne, that was it. Wheeling out M.P.s is normally only done as an eleventh hour thing to try to save a pit under threat, but at Merthyr Vale we were trying to prevent the eleventh hour from happening. We had to emphasise to this new management the importance of the pit and the community. But Wheatley started our meeting by baldly telling us he was a blunt Derbyshire engineer and we came away with an uneasy feeling.'

Then the pit was suddenly put into the review procedure, a death knell sounded by British Coal when they wish to close a pit. Ted Rowlands is convinced that the Welsh Office was caught out by the announcement that Merthyr Vale was to close.

'Peter Walker and the Welsh Office did not have a clue it was going to happen. They were as shocked as me, and it made his earlier assurances that restructuring was over look very ragged. When we appealed to him to help save the pit he gave a standard reply that men could appeal against closure through the review procedure, but then British Coal played their redundancy card. Even Welsh Office minister Ian Grist appealed to Haslem, the head of British Coal, asking them to drop the threat of restructuring redundancy payments.

'I think Peter Walker was particularly embarrassed about it all.

'This was my first real experience of the macho management of British Coal, the first time I realised they weren't accountable to anyone—not to the community not even to government ministers. I believe Wheatley was pursuing a role to eliminate any pit, even if it had long term potential, unless it was going to be extremely profitable. A couple of months losses gave a ground for closure. Deep Navigation (closed at Easter 1991) wasn't even losing money. Everything from then on was done with great speed.'

Ted Rowlands feels that the long term affects of the closure will take years to assess. 'There's a devastating break in tradition—there will never again be a Merthyr Vale sunk in Wales—you'd never get planning permission in this day and age. Just imagine trying to open a pit in a beautiful valley like Merthyr Vale now.

'We won't know the true cost in national terms for some time, only when our energy supplies become the subject of imports. Locally people feel hurt and I think it has shown in their health. The management has no understanding of a community and what it means because if they did they would have to stop and think about what they're doing by closing down pits like this. But, we're great survivors.

'However what British Coal is now going to have to realise is that there is absolutley nil obligation from the community to them any more. They believe they can tread on politicians and communities, but when they try to come back—and they will come back—they'll find the barriers in the community are up and we are not going to be battered into new desolation.

'The blackmailing is over. Villagers in Merthyr Vale and Treharris put up with dust and noise and all sorts of problems while the pit was there because it was so important. Now they've got nothing to blackmail us with; for a change we've got what they want but they're not going to get it.'

Aberfan, 1990

Peter Walker

Peter Walker has been Conservative MP for Worcester since 1961, but is standing down at the next election. In Mrs Thatcher's government he served as Secretary of State for Energy between 1983 and 1987, covering the period of the miners strike, and then became Secretary of State for Wales until May 1990.

'Decisions on pit closures have always been made by British Coal and not the government. There's no warning to any minister when a pit closure takes place. British Coal constantly review the pits and would probably say to the Department of Energy, look, we are informing the men next week that it's our view this pit should be closed. The minister is not responsible for the detailed assessment of whether a pit is economic or not, or what the demand is for coal. That's the job of the coal industry. The only intervention I made, which was a very radical intervention, was in instigating the independent review procedure. Even though the decision would remain with British Coal, it would be quite difficult for them to proceed with any closure against the judgement of an independent arbitrator.'

But miners at Merthyr Vale believe that British Coal's tactics over the timing of the revised redundancy scheme and the announcement of impending closure made a mockery of any possible review. Peter Walker concedes that British Coal could have done more to help the miners and he even wrote to the head of the industry concerning this.

'There was a scheme whereby nobody had to take compulsory redundancy and that was in place for a period of time on terms unmatched by any other industry in Europe. Therefore it may be that the ending of those terms affected the men's decisions. I think it would have been perfectly reasonable for British Coal to say that if you want to go through the review procedure we will, and if at the end of the review we still decide to close the pit, we will stick to the present redundancy terms.'

But he defends British Coal's right to manage and questions whether they were any more accountable to previous Labour governments.

'When dozens of pits were closed in Wales during periods under Labour, did Ted Rowlands think they were accountable then? It was under Alf Robens, a former Labour minister, that dozens and dozens of pits were closed. The coal industry in Wales has declined since 1931, apart from during the war.

'The strike of 1984 didn't help, for during that period many pits were badly damaged and flooded. The coal industry has greatly benefitted in that the electricity industry has purchased its coal in Britain at a much higher cost than it would have had to pay on the international market, so that electricity consumers have to some extent been subsidising coal production. I think there was a justification for that because you can argue there was a security of supply from British Coal. But there were industries that looked upon their own security of supply after the Scargill strike, and instead considered oil, gas or electricity.'

He has no romantic vision of the coal industry. 'For a community and men that have worked in a particular industry, for that industry to come to an end is a very sad thing. However I don't believe the coal industry has been a very happy aspect of the Welsh scene, because apart from being a very rough, very tough industry, it is one that was very badly hit by recessions, it was in constant decline because pits do run out of coal that can be economically mined, and for a time it dominated the opportunities in the valleys and the young in the valleys who didn't want to go into coal. And plenty of them who didn't want to go into coal moved out of the valleys .

'With the inheritance of bad environment, bad pollution, slag heaps and people with very nasty injuries and illnesses it wasn't a good industry. Now at Merthyr Tydfil you see a whole range of new industries, a whole range of new activities, and a whole range of new facilities. I always remember talking to an ex-miner in a new factory and asking him how the two jobs compared. His language was such that he clearly preferred working in the daylight with normal hours and with none of the hazards of the coalfield, and for good pay.'

Peter Walker admits he is concerned about the affects on community life brought about by pit closures. 'The one great thing about mining, though it's true about anything where there's common adversity, was the terrific sense of community and I think everything possible has to be done to retain that sense. But with a diversity of jobs for the young, and the young staying in the valleys instead of leaving the valleys.'

It was with this in mind that he created his valleys initiative. 'Already the coal industry was a minority occupation. But all of the scars of the coal industry were still there, the slag heaps, the dereliction, the pollution of land. And it was a combination of improving buildings, eradicating the pollution of the past, the clearance of derelict land, and putting in a great diversity of housing that has started to give the valleys a new appearance. I hope with the continuation of the initiative that by the turn of the century the valleys will be happier and better.'

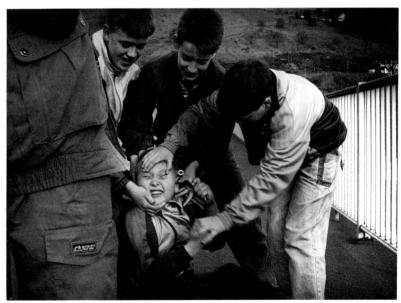

Top left: Gaynor Madgewick and daughter, 1990   Top right: Aberfan cemetery's fundraising committee, 1990
Bottom left: Merthyr Vale from Aberfan cemetery, 1990   Bottom right: Aberfan, 1990

Schoolchildren, Rhymney valley, 1985

Malcolm Aylward

Malcolm's great-grandfather, John Aylward, one of a family of thirteen, came over from Waterford in Ireland to help sink the colliery and worked in the number one pit. His grandfather left school at 14 to go underground, the last 14 year old to be taken on, and his father acted likewise at fifteen. His great-grandfather was killed in the pit when, Malcolm believes, he was run over by a dram. Now aged 42, Malcolm started working in the coal industry on his fifteenth birthday. He spent six weeks training at Aberaman and then went straight into Merthyr Vale. He was the last man to leave the pit.

'When I first started work everybody I knew in the street was at the pit. Four generations of my family had worked there—my great-grandfather was one of those who came from Ireland to open up the pit and it was natural for the rest of the family to follow.'

When the pit closed Malcolm signed on the dole for just one day before he was sent back to supervise the clearing up operation.

'About two months after the pit was closed I was the last man to travel in the cages as I had to cut the cables. When it was my turn to leave I thought it was the end of everything—I thought it was the end of me—twenty years is a long time there.

'Salvage work then went on above ground until 4 May. It was terrible to see what British Coal had left behind; it was unbelievable. Although some things were salvaged I believe millions of pounds worth of equipment was simply buried with the pit. There were thousands of pounds worth of compressors, two winding houses were left as they were, five electric shovels resembling bulldozers worth £30,000 each, £140,000 of equipment in the roadways, and miles of conveyors. Even the face was left as it was with the face cutting machines and haulage houses. Mile upon mile of heavy duty cables was simply abandoned, along with five transformers worth £50,000.

'Only a month before the colliery closed I was instructed to install a mile of electric cable and a new electrical board for the developments which we were told were to take place. So during the miners' holiday I carried out installment work costing well over £40,000 for these so-called new developments.

'After the closure orders were given to seal off the pit as quickly as possible. The two shafts had to be filled by Christmas, four months after the closure. British Coal installed two conveyors and thousands of tons of rock and stone aggregate was poured down the shafts to make sure they could never be opened again. It was a scandal and it made it worse knowing just how much was being buried. I think they were afraid private developers would come along and reopen the mine and make a success of it, causing them great embarrassment.

'I was the last man to come from Merthyr Vale, but now I've seen a different kind of life, a clean job in a factory, and it's a different ball game. The pressure isn't there like it was underground. For years I had been working seven days a week in the pit, but now when I reach home I've finished.'

Malcolm works in a factory in the neighbouring Rhymney Valley which makes tissue culture plant for medical and surgical equipment. 'The pay I'm getting now compares well because I'm working much less hours. Miners on standard pay were getting £170 a week; women are receiving that for a five day week at the factory. I'm in the fresh air all day and it's a good clean job.

'But we still think about the pit, all the cables and tunnels underneath and still talk about it in the pubs at night. In a pit you depend on each other—if somebody had a bump underground you'd carry him two miles to get him up. It's a different life altogether in a factory, the comradeship is just not there.'

Malcolm Aylward, Merthyr Vale, 1990

111

George Jones, Malcolm Aylward's uncle, Aberfan, 1990

Aberfan, 1990

Alf Davies, a former miner, with his rejected pneumonoconiosis claim. Aberfan, 1990

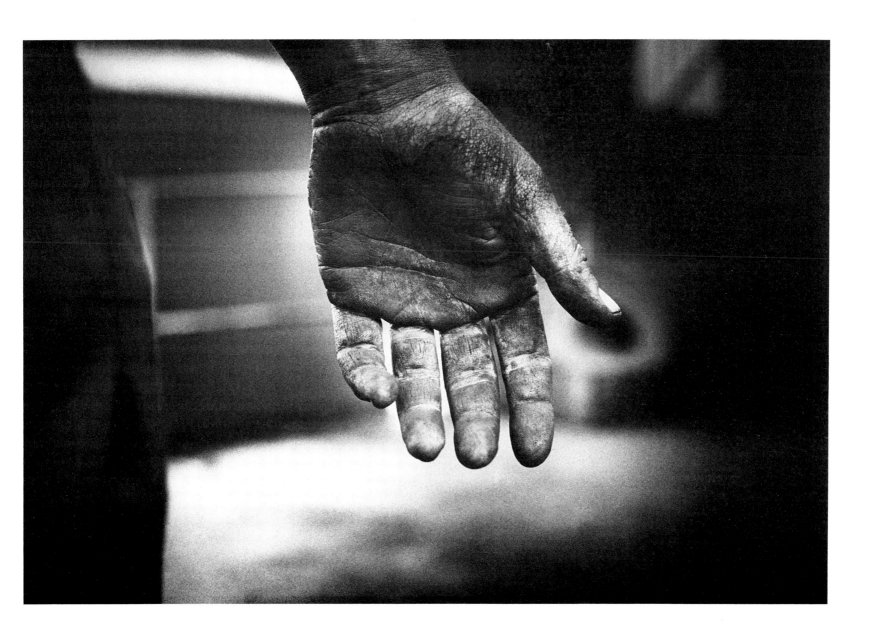

Miner's hand, 1990

Merthyr Vale, 1990

Carl Roberts

Carl's great-grandfather travelled from Blaenau Ffestiniog in North Wales to Merthyr Vale looking for work. The family has never moved from the village since, with Carl's father, now aged 63, going underground at the age of 14, Carl himself starting work with British Coal at the age of 16. After a short training period he too went underground at Merthyr Vale, though not without reservations.

For more than most people living in Aberfan, the colliery has totally dominated Carl's life. Once it almost claimed it, and a second time it robbed him of the only lifestyle he knew.

Carl was only 6 when the tip discard came crashing through the classroom where he had been playing house with his other small classmates. Tucked away in a wendy house in the corner of the room, he suddenly heard a loud rumble and feared, like others, that it was thunder. Within seconds a black sea of slurry had overwhelmed the room, sweeping desks away and smothering him and his friends. Carl was partially buried by the thick slurry, but was spared the waiting ordeal of other children as he was knocked unconscious by a stone and did not come around until he was being carried to safety from the broken school by an old man. To this day he has never been able to find the man who saved him. His father remembers the day well.

'I was overman in charge of our district where about 50 of us were working. The pit mechanic suddenly came up to me and said the tip had come down on the school. Straight away I wanted to know which, and when he said the junior school I knew Carl was there. Every miner just stopped and went there and when I arrived I saw Carl's mother, Bet. She broke the news that our boy was injured but alive, and I then helped through to the next day to try to save the rest of the children.'

For the next twelve years Carl suffered blinding headaches and, until recently, twice a year had to undergo brain scans at a local hospital.

The episode left him with an inbuilt fear of the dark. 'One doctor told me it all probably went back to the time when I was smothered in the disaster—something brought on by what happened to me in that classroom that day.' But despite the fear of the dark and therefore the fear of going underground, Carl was determined to follow in his father's footsteps, and those of the two previous generations.

'I had never even thought of doing anything else. It just never even entered my mind. My father had been bringing home good wages, it was a good job and there was nothing else in the village. It was just natural I should follow. I remember the first day I had to go to the Brittania training school—I was excited but terribly nervous because I've always been shy and nervous of starting new things.' Every miner was sent to Brittania colliery, a fully functional and working pit in the Rhymney valley, for his initial training.

'My first day underground is still as vivid as ever. I had in my box four egg sandwiches and a chocolate wafer bar, but I had to take off the wrapping before I could go under as it had silver paper on it. A spark from the foil could have ignited the fine coal dust and cause an explosion, so it was contraband.

'I had to go down with a training instructor. But I was really frightened for even now, at my age, I won't go anywhere without a light and here I was going right underground. My father had told me what it was like but I did not really know what to expect. It was like waiting for a nightmare; I was sweating and afraid.

'There were about sixteen of us and we had to take the train underground. When we started moving it was like being on a ghost train as you just didn't know what was coming around the next corner. At first everything was pitch black and suddenly we went sweeping down a dip which was like going down a big dipper in the dark. A lot of us were really frightened.'

When Carl actually reached the pit bottom he had the biggest surprise of all. 'It was like the Blackpool illuminations down there. I couldn't believe it, there were lights everywhere. I just breathed a sigh of relief.'

For the next few years Carl's work lay underground. 'Sometimes you would have to walk alone into a dark area and if the chocks supporting the roofs had recently been moved you could hear behind you rocks crashing down from the roof. It was awful as you could hear but not see them. Then there were the rats. I never saw one the whole time I was underground, but I knew they were lurking there and the thought used to give me goose pimples.'

His father also recalls the rats. 'Of course there were no toilets or anywhere to eat, so you just stopped where you were to go to the toilet and you had just twenty minutes to eat your food wherever you stopped. There were still pit ponies underground taking supplies up, but the feed from the stables underground used to attract rats, which were swarming all over the place. But it's strange, there's always been an old saying that where there are mice you won't find rats and that's exactly what happened. When we broke through to the area being coaled by Deep Navigation, to provide an emergency escape route, our rats disappeared. Deep

Navigation had been overrun by mice and us by rats, but after we broke through we never saw the rats again. They vanished, but it was then the crickets came.'

Later Carl was given a job on the surface in the lamp room where he spent his last eight years working at the mine. 'I absolutely loved my job there, it was all I ever wanted. I worked six days a week every week, sometimes going in on a Sunday, and although I wasn't earning what you could underground, I was bringing home £150.'

Carl was one of the miners who fought for the pit to be saved and voted for the men to go through the review procedure. When that was voted down, he felt he could not face a transfer so decided to take redundancy and look for a new career. After fourteen years in the pit his redundancy money amounted to a total of £6,400.

'I know a lot of the older miners who normally would have voted to save the pit voted for closure because they were frightened of losing their redundancy money. British Coal had frightened us all into believing that if we didn't accept the closure by 26 August, we would receive nothing.'

Carl soon learnt that they would have been better off fighting through the review procedure, a tactic which would have given them more time at the pit. A friend of his who started at Merthyr Vale colliery just a month before him decided to transfer to Deep Navigation colliery a few miles away. In December 1989 his friend decided to take redundancy after British Coal appealed for volunteers and received a redundancy payment of £18,000.

'I just can't understand why they closed Merthyr Vale. We were doing so much better than other pits and had a much brighter future. It was the awful way we were treated that hurt. Men who had put in thirty-two years of service were even refused the concessionary coal for which they had worked all their lives for their old age, because they were just short of reaching the entitlement age of 50.'

But worse was to follow. Carl soon found that his work in the pit had given him few useful skills with which to obtain other work.

He went along to British Coal Enterprise and decided to take up the offer of training to become a heavy goods vehicle driver. 'It was just another big disappointment and let down. I was told that I would have to find a haulage firm to sponsor me to train and take my test and that if I was successful British Coal Enterprise would pay back their money. I tried everywhere, even a friend, but who was going to take such a big gamble on me when the outlay was £1,000. It was impossible.' He wasn't happy to use any of his redundancy pay as he saw that as protecting his family's future. If he failed the test he would have lost £1,000.

No Noise just silence.
No jobs are seen.
No turning wheels,
No trams can move,
No banging or driving lorries.
No JCBs.
Just silence!
It's not the same.
It's just not the same.

Don Sorday, Ynysowen school

Now the pit is closing down,
All machinery underground.
Silence reigns, quiet cranes.
No more dirt,
no more hurt.
Goodbye pit,
you'll be missed a bit
from the valley around.
Goodbye men, see you again.

David Davis, Ynysowen school

Carl then joined a government backed job club where he wrote to and telephoned forty different employers seeking work. Most applications went unanswered, but he did obtain two interviews, one with the water authority and one with Thorn lighting. Neither was successful.

'There was nothing offering anything near the type of pay I was getting in the colliery. There were jobs offering £82 a week, but you had to travel away, whereas I was able to claim £75 from social security. I was also told I could apply for a milkman's job in Newport thirty miles away, but that would have meant getting up at 3 every morning. There were plenty of jobs for the skilled miners, electricians and people like that, but nobody wanted the likes of me.'

He was eventually accepted onto a City and Guilds car mechanics course sponsored by Mid Glamorgan County Council and received an extra £10 a week on top of his social security and which paid for the travelling.

His father finds the whole episode saddening. 'It's terrible to see a young boy like mine, young men of thirty with young families and no jobs to go to. When I went down it was automatic that you went down the pit and your son followed you. I wanted Carl's son, my grandson, Jason, to go underground. It was a good job. Goodness knows what will happen to him now. I fear that he and other youngsters from the village will be forced to move away as there's nothing else for them. There's no work here.

'He'll probably end up like everybody else in a small factory unit in another valley. It's really sad for he'll be the first after four generations not to work in the village pit and to keep the tradition going.'

Merthyr Vale, 1990

Merthyr Vale, 1990

122

Mother and child, 1991

Grandfather and grandson, Treharris, 1990

124

Above Treharris, 1990

Deep Navigation, 1990

126

Showers. Top left: Merthyr Vale, 1990   Top right: With Ted Rowlands (centre), Merthyr Vale
        Bottom left: Merthyr Vale, 1990   Bottom right: Deep Navigation, 1990

'The Magnificent Seven' The last miners on safety work, Merthyr Vale, 1990

Russell John

Russell John started with the National Coal Board when he left school at the age of 16. His grandfather, William Lewis, had worked underground all his life, dying from pneumonoconiosis and tuberculosis when his father, Ivor, was a small boy. Ivor had worked at Ogilvie colliery in the Rhymney valley before it closed and he transferred to Merthyr Vale. Ivor will never work again, although he's only in his early fifties, as he suffers from deafness and dizziness caused by underground blasting. Russell's brother Nigel, his elder by two years, did not like the atmosphere at Merthyr Vale as he felt the pit was being run down in preparation for closure and transferred to Deep Navigation. Here he was treated as an outsider and a new boy because he'd come from a different pit, a common problem on transfer. He stayed for just twelve months and is now unemployed.

'"You must promise me you'll never go down the pit"—those were the first words I ever remember my grandfather saying to me. I was sitting on my grandfather's bed where he was laying, dying from pneumonoconiosis and TB brought on from years of working underground. As he lay in bed he was on oxygen and was determined we shouldn't follow in his footsteps and go through the agonies he'd suffered. He was really bitter about it all and used to go on at our mother all the time not to let us go underground.

'My mother was also really upset as she didn't want us to go to work in a pit. She used to try to stop us but in the end it seemed the natural thing to do to to follow my father underground. There was no other real choice for me anyway. I had thrown away my chances in school where I rebelled against the system and got expelled in the last year, and so left with no qualifications. The pit was the most attractive option left. I was guaranteed a job because my father had worked in the mine and was well respected, and the money they were offering was good.

'Even now I think back on my grandfather's words and think if my two children waste the opportunities being offered through education I would kill them. But even so I don't regret for one minute going underground. I wouldn't have missed it for a million pounds as it's the best learning experience you can ever have. Unless you've worked underground where you're putting your life in someone's hands and are depending on others for your own safety you could never understand the very special comradeship that is built up between miners. The loyalty is something you won't experience anywhere else.

'Somehow the first time you go underground you are proving you're a man. I remember young boys who wouldn't wash their faces properly in the showers—going home with eyes like panda bears just to prove they were now working underground and were men. When we first started training, people would trail their hands in the dust to get their faces dirty to look like proper miners. If someone did that now you'd shout at them—they'd just be causing problems with dust and threatening your health.'

His first day, as for most young miners, was bewildering. He knew none of the faces he encountered although most men, because of his father, knew who he was. Russell remembers the pride miners felt as they started off with a white band around their lamps on their helmets to signify they were just beginning. The white was progressively replaced by a yellow and then a red lamp signifying their seniority and high rank.

He also remembers most vividly and with most regret the days when he went to work in the dark and came home in the dark. 'From September to early spring there were times when you didn't really see daylight properly at all. It would make you really depressed, for you'd go out in the dark in the morning and even before the light had come up you'd be underground. By the time you came back up, had a shower, got home and had your tea, it was dark again. You seemed to be living in a permanent darkness.

'I'd get up at 5.30 to catch a bus near my home twenty minutes later and would then go straight to the lamp room for a 7 o'clock start. On my last job I'd have to walk about three-quarters of a mile underground, the way ahead lit only by my lamp, to the lamp station where I would sit on the floor and have one of my sandwiches. That was breakfast, as nobody ever started until they'd had something to eat there. If I was working at one of the furthest headings I would then have to load the journey of trams with heavy timber and metal supports. That was really heavy work. Then I'd face another mile long walk up a steep gradient to the heading.

'I'd stay underground in the darkness all day until my shift finished mid-afternoon and I'd have to walk all the way back. The conditions at times were really bad. Sometimes we were working in twelve inches of water and you can imagine what it's like to work and eat in the same place where men had to go to the toilet.

'It was then quickly into the showers and a quick change to make sure you caught the bus home. Very often by the time I got in and had something to eat it was dark and I was just exhausted. When I was single every night after work I would go out to the pub or club with other miners, but since I've been married that's all stopped and I don't go out after work any more.'

Russell had always been regarded as a militant with strong socialist views, but he believes the miners strike not only expanded his beliefs but also helped mellow them.

He started the strike helping picket collieries in Staffordshire and Leicester. 'My brother was arrested on a picket line in Staffordshire and was later convicted of affray. Thousands of miners who had never been in trouble before were convicted simply because of their beliefs and their fight for a job during the strike.' Russell in turn was arrested on a demonstration in London, but was later found not quilty of assaulting a policeman. Meanwhile he helped picket Didcot power station, but on his way back from the picket one day he ran into a local fracas unconnected with the strike.

'As I tried to keep clear of the disturbance I ran straight into a motorbike and broke my leg. Although I was in agony for weeks it was all worth while because it was through my broken leg that I met my wife. I didn't want to be stuck in a hospital in Oxford away from my family and most friends for sixteen weeks and asked to be transferred nearer home. So after just one night I was sent to the Prince Charles Hospital in Merthyr where I met Debbie who was there as a nurse. We married soon after.'

Time spent lying in hospital gave him time to mull over recent events. 'The strike changed my attitude to many things. I have never looked on the police with the same eyes—how can you when you've seen coppers waving their pay slips at you when they know you haven't got a penny.

'It also changed my political outlook. I'd always been extremely militant but for the first time in my life I met with groups from all different political persuasions. 'I even met one agitator who said he was a socialist, but he was like a general. It was a case of we'll issue you the guns and you, the miners, can go off and fight. They were from a different planet as they didn't have any experience of real life at all. I told one he should come and see what it was like on a picket line, see that very often there was no excitement, just routine, getting cold and hungry but although he was preaching revolution he didn't come.'

The day that British Coal announced that the pit was being reviewed, he says the atmosphere underground completely changed. 'From that day I knew that the pit did not have a single chance of being saved. I simply gave up hoping, knowing it was all a game of bluff and I didn't want to play. My heart completely went out of the job and for that last twelve months there's no way I accepted it could be saved. Many thought it had a future, but I had no doubt it would close.

'At the end it was just a gipsy pit—there were miners from as many as five other mines there and they had all been through other pit closures and feared the worst. The new targets they set were impossible, but many of the men just gave everything to try to save the pit. The only thing that wasn't given in my opinion was a life. I'm surprised that in those last few months no one was killed underground, for people were taking really big chances just to try to improve production. I saw times when there were no safety precautions being taken at all; they were thrown to the wind. People were literally putting their lives at risk to try to save the jobs and the pit. Those last twelve months were awful, the most miserable of my life.'

Russell was one of the miners who voted for the pit to close, believing that whatever action the men took the pit was finished. 'It couldn't have gone on much longer. Older miners say there were plenty of reserves but I think geologically it was shut. Even heavy duty chocks were beginning to snap under the strain underground.

'But at the end it was awful. We voted in the morning and in the afternoon were told our jobs no longer existed and to go home. Most of us went straight over to the Gordon's club and got drunk. All I felt was a great sense of relief it was finally over, but others at the pub were really unhappy about it all. Many of the men were really angry and there was abuse flying because people disagreed over whether we should have voted to fight or close. But at the end of the day everybody respected each other's opinion so that was that.

'I think my father must have been upset about the way I voted. But I thought it was just stupidity to carry on fighting British Coal which wasn't going to change its mind. To me it was a godsend it closed when it did before somebody died trying to save it.'

For the first time in his life Russell had to try to find a job. He first signed on with a firm in Pontypridd as a financial representative—a glorified insurance salesman. He had to sell twelve policies before he could earn a guaranteed wage of £400 a month and was advised to phone around his family first to try to sell the policies. After a week he left to become a vacuum cleaner salesman in Cardiff. He was quickly trained in high pressure sales techniques to try to sell the machines at £800 each.

'Again I was told to try to sell to my friends first and was told to use high pressure sales techniques even on old people. I was trained to vacuum clean people's beds, then spill the contents out onto a piece of black velvet and show them they were sleeping in slums which would create a serious health hazard. Women used to say things like "What if my neighbour ever found out" and would buy these machines. But after spending all my life in a proper job I just couldn't do it for very long.'

After a week he left and, after failing to get into the fire brigade, remained unemployed until the following April.

In April he started work in the Sun Valley chicken factory where he had to joint and strip thousands of cooked chickens a day. After working virtually on his door-step all his life Russell and some friends from the mine now faced a round journey of 85 miles a day to Hereford, and he spent a reasonable part of his £4,500 redundancy money on buying a second hand car.

'It was all a huge shock. I'd never even carved a chicken before then. When I started work that day it was like walking onto another planet. After all those years underground in a real job there I was standing in line dressed in a pinny, a hair net and wellington boots stripping chicken carcasses.

'That first morning I was bewildered and I could barely cope with it. There were supervisors above me who thought that they were really important and I wasn't used to that attitude. People would cut you up to get overtime, if you'd done that in a pit you'd have been done over. There just wasn't that comradeship that I had been used to. No longer were people relying on you for their lives and you weren't dependent on them.'

A typical day mystfied him. 'When you get into the factory you have to put on a pair of surgical slippers, take out a pair of wellingtons in a sterile bag and then scrub and sterilise your hands. You then put on a hairnet and hat and go on into the sterile area. Here you would put on the sterile wellingtons, go through a sterile well-ington bath, wash your hands again and put on a pinny, rubber glove liners on your hands and then the rubber gloves. You'd then have to wash again, something you did every quarter of an hour thereafter.

'To someone who'd worked in a mine where men had to go to the toilet where they stood it was like being in a different world. The only way I could get through it was to keep my mouth shut and try to do the work. I switched my mind off and resembled a robot, as I knew I had to carry on as my wife was pregnant with our second child, and I needed the money.'

Within weeks Russell's fingers had started to seize up from the delicate work and the handling of the chilled chickens, and he had to have physiotherapy for arthritis.

After six weeks unable to stand the job any longer he was transferred to the dispatch department and later moved to a factory nearer home at Abergavenny.

A year after the pit closed and more settled Russell says his move out of the pit was the best thing he ever did. 'Now I am perfectly happy. I see more of the daylight and I am glad the pit has closed. This job is a hell of a lot easier and I'm bringing home about the same pay, but even so it's still strange and I miss colliery life.

'When I think now of my grandfather's words I think the eight years underground were the best years of my life except for that time when we were under threat. But I was lucky, I've got a job that I now enjoy. Other men's lives revolved completely around the pit. That's all they lived and breathed for, they went to work and went out with miners in the night. For them it's been really difficult.'

Top left: The site of Merthyr Vale colliery, 1991   Top right: Clearing up, Merthyr Vale colliery, 1991
Bottom left: Aberfan, 1991   Bottom right: Merthyr Vale, 1991

Coal delivery, Merthyr Vale, 1991

Demolition man, Merthyr Vale colliery site, 1991

137

Dismantling Merthyr Vale colliery, 1991

Men taking away the last of the colliery pieces, Merthyr Vale, 1991

Aberfan, 1990

Andrew Leonard, Aberfan, 1990

Aberfan, 1990

Whereas before, governments used to give subsidies to carry out loss making operations, the pits were then exposed to the full force of market pressures. Collieries had to compete with coal traded on world markets and unless they could produce at an economic cost they couldn't survive. The problem with pits like Merthyr Vale was that the best of the coal was worked out a long time ago, leaving the reserves further away.

Mike Meredith

The leaders of British Coal seem to have a perverse desire to close every pit. It's as if their only ambition is to terminate the whole of the South Wales coalfield. That's wrong. Wrong for the area and wrong for Britain too.

Neil Kinnock

How heartless can they be. You just look up at the graves above you and see the price people have paid for coal—they've paid a price second to none. They have taken away the jobs of brothers who lost brothers and sisters in the disaster and even the jobs of their fathers. How could they do it?

Tony Davies

I think it was very bad to close Merthyr Vale. There were plenty of reserves. But if it hadn't been the pit associated with Aberfan I think it would have closed years before—they were just frightened of the public reaction.

Terry Donoghue

I was really surprised when they closed Merthyr Vale because of what had happened in Aberfan and I thought that that alone would have kept it open. In my opinion there was a maximum of three years coaling left, but they could have let it die a natural death. But if the country no longer wants coal, what could British Coal do. The pit producing it at the most expensive rate must go to the wall and when you consider they were closing wonderful pits in England which had excellent reserves it was inevitable pits in Wales would have to go.

Graham Schewitz

I think it was indecent the way they closed the pit leaving millions of pounds worth of equipment underground. It's obscene when you think about what they did. The men deserved better than that.

Carl Roberts

A new beginning?

When it came to the end it was no good fighting. The pit was already closed as far as Hobart House was concerned, but instead of letting it die a death they decapitated it straight away.

Ray Tovey

I was really sorry to hear of the pit's closure. They had gone through so much and ended up without a pit—where their fathers and grandfathers had worked before them. If one struggles for something and has an honest belief in that struggle, then that belief must be respected.

Glyn Rogers

Everything is changing here now and the pit closure has just added to what's happening. I can go a week before I even see my next door neighbour. Strangers are moving into the village and it's really changing.

Suzie Evans

I would have liked to have seen much more of a fight put up, but in the end it had to be the miners' decision. It wasn't for me to say although my great-grandfather and my grandfathers had worked there, it was for those working there to decide. Only time will tell if they made the right or wrong decision and what will happen in the community. We are not going to stop being a community just because the colliery has closed.

Maureen Hughes

We have already fought our bit, we've been through those hard times, going short of food and everything else. We fought to have something better, now it's up to the younger ones. But I wonder how future families are going to fare.

I'm worried that it's going to revert to the days we experienced in the 1920's and 30's, and that people will get poorer and poorer. But the biggest worry is that all the young people will leave the area like we did before the war. We weren't the only ones. A lot of youngsters left Aberfan and Merthyr Vale at that time desperate for work. We came back but what will the youngsters have to come back to.

Doris Richards

South Wales Pit Closures

1985
Celynen North, Newbridge
Blaensychan, Pontypool
Bedwas, Caerphilly
Celynen South, Newbridge
Markham, Blackwood
Treforgan, Neath
Aberpergwm, Glyn-Neath
Penrhiwceiber, Mountain Ash
Abertillery
St John's, Maesteg
Garw/Ffaldau, Bridgend

1986
Coed Ely, Llantrisant
Nantgarw, Taffs Well
Cwm/Coed Ely, Pontypridd

1988
Lady Windsor/Abercynon, Ynysybwl
Abernant, Pontardawe
Six Bells, Abertillery

1989
Cynheidre, Llanelli
Marine, Ebbw Vale
Oakdale
Merthyr Vale
Trelewis Drift

1990
Blaenant

1991
Deep Navigation

Merthyr Vale, 1990

145

Demolition man, Merthyr Vale, 1991

Closure parade for Deep Navigation colliery, Treharris, 1991

Social club, Merthyr Vale, 1990

Top left: Aberfan, 1990   Top right: Merthyr Vale, 1990
Bottom left: Rhymney valley, 1985   Bottom right: Merthyr Vale, 1990

Russell John and baby, 1991

Aberfan, 1990

151

Aberfan, 1991

152

1907

Mar	John Evans of Neath killed in No2 pit.
Mar 25	Board of Governors election. A notice board was placed on the wall of Fire Office urging all workmen to vote for the timekeeper a hankering-scoundrel namely, Richard Rees, by order of Michael and Benjamin Thomas. Such is our official tyranny, issued by two ink flashing jackasses.
May 7	I planted against the oak tree here, an ivy creeper about 8 feet high, and its base one inch diameter.
May 9	Griffith Williams of Oakland killed in No 1 pit. Edwin Gough seriously injured at the same time and place.
May 12	Mr. Duggan labourer of Perthygleision farm found unconscious near the Magazine, exposed to the weather all night. Died shortly afterwards, buried at Aberfan cemetery.
May	Rain and rough weather, as not been approached for a period of seventy years.
June	Like the preceding month.
June 15	Trial of new washery plant, which replaces the one burnt down on Nov 3 1906. Estimate damage at £1,200.
June 20	So very cold that exposed fingers were soon numbed.
June 21	Great thunder also rain and hail storms. Such were the torrents of rain that many a score of houses were flooded. The hail-stones were exceedingly large. With a girdle around the centre, which perforated nearly the whole glass roofing in this place. At Blaen-nant-y-Fedw farm two dogs were killed and two boys had a narrow escape.
Aug 28	Women of Crescent and Taff Street arrested and threw turf at the non unionists.
Aug 29	Great reinforcement of policemen.
Aug 30	Greater reinforcement of policemen.
Sep 7	The first professional Rugby Football match played in Wales (Merthyr versus Oldham) at Merthyr Tydfil.
Sep 12	Harry Everson at one time a Smith's mate here saved the life of a sinker at Penallta (recommended for the King's Medal).
Sep 17	Great meeting of women at Aberfan Hall re non Unionist. Mrs Williams wife of John Williams carpenter, died from shock brought about by the drunken antics of her son.

The Ledger

Written by William John of Merthyr Vale who died in 1925, the ledger has been kept by his grandson Eddie John, a third generation miner and who's son in turn became a miner.

Sep 30	William Williams son of the above Mrs. Williams was killed at No1 pit. This person was mainly responsible for the death of his mother. Here in this case I think we have 'God' punishing the guilty. On this day he returned to work and was in the act of filling the first tram when a large stone struck him on the back of his neck, death being instantaneous.
Nov 1	County Council election. David Jones check-weigher returned by 36 votes. A great surprise for the 'Hawks' who reckoned their man Benjamin Morgan Thomas (casher) would be returned.
Nov 7	7 per cent bank rate. The highest rate since the year 1873.
Nov	This month on the whole has been a very mild one. Strawberries, raspberries and gooseberries grow in the open in different parts of Wales.
Dec 2	Ebenezer Edmunds (a white worker in lime) met his death in the eighteen inch pipe in the Havod Tanglas Brook.
Dec 8	Mrs. Thomas Aubrey of Dandydarren died through the wilful neglect of a lazy husband.
Dec 9	Mrs. Marther Davies of Tylan (corpse) was carried by men to Gelliger Cemetery (in dreadful weather).
Dec 12	Mr. George Cavill and Mrs. Jane Cavill of Forrest House Merthyr Vale are now bound over in their own recognizance of £20 each to appear at the Cardiff Quarter Sessions for cruel and wilful neglect to a young lad, a nephew of theirs by name Lionel Hopkins.
	The inhabitants of Merthyr Vale and Troedyrhiw are in a waxen state of human wroth over the Cavill case. To think that an uncle and aunt would so conspire, to such revolting cruelty, which if it had its course for a few more years would result in the death of this poor orphan boy. She! this she-devil being the next of kin would consequently in the event of his death claim the property. This case is the most scandalous of its kind to living knowledge in the Merthyr district.
Dec 14	An explosion in the Dinas main colliery, Gilfach Goch. Seven poor fellows killed.
Dec 25	A day which was wet and dreary both morning and afternoon. A Christmas of the 'greenest hue' the blades of grass appear as green as in the springtime, and few of our mature plants appear with withered leaves. At Penddaugae Fawr farm there are still to be seen butter-cups and daisies in full bloom.

1908

Jan 16   Jack Lad and co of the Ariel rope-way sent down an ultimatum written on a shovel, in the following words. 'If you do not send us that whisky up soon we shall go on strike.' The management soon complied with their request.

Jan 19   An organised conspiracy of a sleek and secret nature took place on 6 Jan 1908. The employers at Treharris, Merthyr Vale, Hills Plymouth, Cyfarthfa and Dowlais instructed their officials from the lower to the higher order to present themselves at the town hall Merthyr Tydfil and vote amass against the corporation's Water scheme. Needless to state the conspirators defeated the water scheme.

Jan 24   Cromwell Davies age 3 and a half years son of James Davies, 42 Taff Street has been missing since 5 p.m.

Jan 26   The streets of Merthyr on a Sunday night between the hours of 6.30 and 7.30 p.m. appear melancholy in the extreme. An occasional ripple of laughter from the cooing couples of the rag-tag element who parade in the town is the only sentiment intermingled with the hollow sounds of footsteps that jerks you from the idea that you are in the city of the dead.

          After the hour of 7.30 there appeared a transformation in its streets. Thousands are there now assembled from high places of worship whose architecture in many cases cannot be seen from the High Street. The people in the majority of cases are dressed in black bothers, and if the night is wet hundreds by hundreds of umbrellas break the air and collars are hurriedly turned to protect the sham fashions of the throat.

          The light drapery coloured mackintosh is much in vogue with the 'Slinky Aristocrats.' These unsightly overalls look like a large sheet of garish packing paper in a wet condition. Large numbers of young men upon leaving these places of worship, make straight way for the different establishment of the Berni Brothers, and to other foreigners of a same calibre. Here they intermingle the 'Dammed Sinners' and the 'Sinners to the Dammed'. All restaurants and shops which trade in streets confined to British enterprise are closed on Sunday.

          The great rendezvous of the inhabitants and of course that of the visitors is the GWR station. Long before the departure of the evening train, crowds gather under the scantling of this sort of dark and unkempt station.

Jan 26   No clue of the missing lad Cromwell Davies.

Jan 26   All sections of the community searching the district.

Jan 27   Five hundred miners returned from pit top to join in the search.

Jan 28   2.15 p.m. diver William Quick arrived here from Cardiff to search the river's pools.

Jan 29   After two days search of no avail the diver and his three assistants returned to Cardiff by an evening train. This evening a crowded meeting was held in the Drill Hall which decided on a sixpenny 'levy' to protect furher searching.

Jan 30   Forty men, in two sections under the leadership of Mr. Reynold Thomas and Mr. Harry Evans. One section entrained for Abercynon to meet their co-searchers from Merthyr Vale. Likewise other tracks of the river were searched until its whole length from Merthyr Vale to Cardiff was right as rain.

Feb 2   Large meeting in connection with the Boy Mystery.

Feb 5   Search abandoned until the arrival of Capt Byfield.

Feb 6   Mrs. Hopkins of Aberfan died. Sad to state that a very attractive young woman should die more or less through the kicks and blows delivered by her husband, who three months ago went to America.

Feb 9   Sunday, another mass meeting held at the Drill Hall whereat it was decided to requisition the services of the Carmarthen fisher-men with their coracles.

Dust Chamber of no avail (practically useless). Therefore 'they' had no alternative but to discontinue the use of the blower. The greatest nuisance to which the inhabitants of Merthyr Vale and Aberfan has been subject to. Our villages were enshrouded in dust, particles from the minute to a hard-pea size; descending from the wind quarter to adorn our garments, and to friction your eyes a 'Bloody Bed' (this dust laid two feet deep here and there).

Feb 10   Another trait of the new-woman has sprung up amongst us, namely, 'Top-whipping'. Drab girls of 16 and 17 years of age are seen in that particular stoop typical to boys; when having a top under the head. The sight at first fires you with indignation, then later with a calmer survey the different colours which the fringe of their underclothing shows in sight, with the different coloured frocks, and jacket, which they are accustonmed to wear throws up in marked contrast to the usually drab attire of our boys. The whole intermingling with each other in this Top pastime forms a pretty picture with an evil-setting.

Mar 7   Trial trip on my bicycle.

Mar 9   Isaac Evans (young cobbler) locomotive stopper received a serious injury to his foot, by a wagon in motion.

Mar 13   Poor Isaac Evans had his leg amputated at Merthyr Hospital two inches below the knee.

Mar 14   Wales has won the Triple Crown in rugby football.

Apr 6   Asquith as Prime Minister, introduced in his budget, Old-Age Pensions for persons 70 years old.

Apr 28   David Parry of Cross Street Aberfan 'broke' into the house occupied by Andrew Jones with felonious intent for which he received fourteen days imprisonment.

             A new religious order has appeared here, namely the Christian Israelities.

June 16   A great women's demonstration took place at the Aberfan Hall in favour of the Licensing Bill.

July 7   The annual sheep-shearing with my friends at Penddaugae Fawr. I may here note that these shearing days are the most important events among our mountain farmers. They help each other for miles around as in this instance sixteen pairs of shears were kept busily to the sound of click! click!, there were two persons wool packing, another placing pitch marks, one man catching sheep in the pen, and two men driving sheep to pen as required; with three hoop making, a total of twenty five persons. Concerts are held in the night.

Aug 3   The Merthyr Vale male Voice Choir won the first prize of £20 and a chair at the Penycraig Eisteddfod.

Aug 4   The Merthyr Vale male Voice Choir won the first prize of £20 and a baton at the Tonypandy Eisteddfod.

Aug 21   Isaac Jones of 32 Thomas Street, Aberfan, attempted to murder his wife and a lodger by cutting their throat with a pen-knife. He afterwards cut his own throat with a razor. The doctor was soon in attendance and sowed the gap with six stitches. During this operation, Isaac told Dr. White in a vicious tone 'You're an awkward old bugger too.' The doctor retorted 'You're an awkward old bugger too or you would have killed yourself.'

The family of this man seem to be unreal. His cousin Cadwalader Jones murdered his fiancée whom he had got into trouble, by cutting her body into several portions and throwing the parts into the river at Dolgelly; where he was hanged in the year 1882. The wife of his brother T Jones, Crescent Street, Merthyr Vale, tried to kill her daughter and herself from the effects of which she died a few months afterwards.

Oct 1   The establishment of the penny post rate between England and America. I posted the first letter, with a penny stamp affixed from this place, to my friend David Rees.

Oct 19   The greatest rain storm for many years. Extensive damage in several districts. At Bedlinog the culvert of Nantillinog became blocked causing the stream to over run the road. James Williams alias Jim Kelly met his death by being carried away with the flood.

Oct 29   Mrs. Mary O'Leary received serious injuries in following her employment as a washer-woman at No1 Clive Place 'The Barracks or Breeding Cages.' In performinmg her duty the bottom of the balcony suddenly disappeared and poor Mary was found unconscious below.

Dec 7   Thomas Hamer of Aberfan has removed to the old ancient Star Inn at Merthyr. The family of the Star Inn, although freeholders, have gone to the mire of degradation. Like several families of publicans in this district.

Bibliography

The Fed, A History of the South Wales Miners in the Twentieth Century by Hywel Francis and David Smith. Lawrence and Wishart 1980

The Miners Strike in Oxford by the Oxford Miners Support Group. Oxford and District Trades Union Council Miners Support Group 1985

South Wales Miners, A History of the South Wales Miners' Federation 1914 to 1926 by R. Page Arnot. Cymric Federation Press 1975

The Historic Taf Valleys, volume III by John Perkins, Clive Thomas and Jack Evans. The Merthyr and District Naturalists Society in conjunction with D. Brown and sons ltd, Cowbridge 1986

Striking Back. The Welsh Campaign for Civil and Political Liberties and by the NUM 1985

The Life of John Nixon, Pioneer of the Steam Coal Trade in South Wales by James Edmund Vincent. John Murray 1900

The Militancy of British Miners by V.L. Allen. The Moor Press 1981

Report of the Tribunal appointed to inquire into the disaster at Aberfan. HMSO 1967

A Brief History of Merthyr Tydfil by Joseph Gross. The Starling Press Ltd, 1980

Other books from Logaston Press

Alfred Watkins - A Herefordshire Man
By Ron Shoesmith, Hereford city's archaeologist, this book chronicles the life of the author of The Old Straight Track the book which gave birth to Ley Lines. Watkins dabbled in much, inventing the first exposure meter and the book includes over 45 of his own photographs. ISBN 0 9510242 7 2

The Burton Court Recipes - English Food from Herefordshire
By Helen J. Simpson this book includes over 70 traditional and not so traditional recipes using nettles, marigolds, beef, cider, eels, bream, chestnuts, soft fruit, pork, lamb, damsons, cheese, walnuts and much besides. ISBN 1 873827 00 8

Walks & More
By Andrew Johnson & Stephen Punter this is an illustrated guide book to an area from Llandrindod and Builth Wells to the River Severn, from Ross and Ledbury in the south to Stourport and Ludlow in the north. With 80 circular walks, chapters on history, agriculture, folkore, cider, beer and art and literature, and a gazetteer to over 150 towns and villages. ISBN 0 9510242 6 4

The Humble-Bee, Its Life History and How to Domesticate It
By F.W.L. Sladen. Originally published in 1912 and still a classic work, Sladen enthusiastically weaves together the strands of a simple story of natural history and those of profound scholarship in a way accessible to young and old. This edition includes a copy of Sladen's original hand-written monograph of 1892. ISBN 0 9510242 3 X

Also:
The Happy Farmers by Sheila Wenham
Aspects of Herefordshire by Andrew Johnson & Stephen Punter
Aspects of Worcestershire by Andrew Johnson & Stephen Punter
Ludford Bridge & Mortimer's Cross by Geoffrey Hodges
Walks in Southern Powys & the Borders by Andrew Johnson